Everything You Need To Know To Stay Married And Like It

Everything You Need To Know To Stay Married And Like It

by Bennard R. Wiese
and Urban G. Steinmetz

ZONDERVAN PUBLISHING HOUSE
OF THE ZONDERVAN CORPORATION
GRAND RAPIDS, MICHIGAN 49506

EVERYTHING YOU NEED TO KNOW TO STAY MARRIED AND LIKE IT!

Second printing 1974

Library of Congress Catalog Card No. 77-189586

Printed in the United States of America

Contents

Preface
1. Marriage Is Real 11
2. A Formula for Building Love in the Home . . . 26
3. Thinking About Talking 39
4. Improving Communication 50
5. A Complicated Me 61
6. The Many Meanings of Sexual Intercourse . . . 76
7. Thinking About Sexual Intercourse 91
8. The Total Climax of Love 106
9. Plan Ahead: Some Thoughts on Contraception . . 118
10. What Is an Adult? 132
11. The Root of All Evil: Money Matters in Marriage . 143
12. Child Rearing – Freedom With Responsibility . . 154
13. Sex Education in the Home 174
14. Toward a Relevant Morality: What Our Kids Need to Know 187

Bibliography 206
Index 214

Preface

Everything You Need to Know to Stay Married and Like It was inspired by the "Marriage Enrichment" tapes and records written and narrated by Urban G. Steinmetz, Executive Director of the Family Enrichment Bureau, Escanaba, Michigan. I began using the series in my Marriage and Family classes at Northwestern College, Orange City, Iowa, about six years ago and suddenly found that the class size increased rapidly from semester to semester. From others who had taken the course hundreds of students got the word that finally on the campus there was a course which was relevant. Here was a course that dealt with the realities of two persons living together in marriage and that helped them to prepare, if they were not already married, for marriage as a creative experience; and for those who were already married, it helped them to enrich their marital experience. From the already married, I heard many, many times: "If only we had had the opportunity to discuss these important materials before."

The tapes and records alone were extremely interesting, helpful, and stimulating. However, for many it was impossible to assimilate all of the necessary concepts through listening to them only once, even when the major ideas were discussed together in the classroom after listening to each tape or record. Many students checked out the materials to listen to them over and over again by themselves or with their potential mates. Still there was a persistent request for a script or a discussion of the concepts that they could retain permanently in their possession for review and renewal. Consequently, I decided to edit the tapes, to put them into script form to meet this need.

The first eight chapters, plus chapters ten, twelve, and thirteen, are an edited discussion of the "Marriage Enrichment Program," prepared and narrated by Urban G. Steinmetz. They include the newer concepts of the later "Adult Seminar" and the editor's insights and analysis. Chapters nine, eleven, and fourteen are additional discussions of the concepts I consider very important and which have come out of my experience in discussions with college students and marriage counseling sessions in the community. Although Urban G. Steinmetz did not actively participate in the preparation of this manuscript, I am deeply indebted to him for the inspiration that made this work possible and for his and the Family Enrichment Bureau's gracious permission to use many of the perceptive concepts and insights which have been previously copyrighted by himself and the Family Enrichment Bureau as recorded and taped programs. I also owe a great deal to many other authors, the participants at many conferences, to my students, and to my wife and children. Many of the ideas, phrases, sentences, and concepts have long lost their specific identity as they were integrated into my own thought pattern and class presentations.

But why another book on marriage? Don't we already have enough? When one looks over the library shelves, he might easily come to the conclusion that adequate materials are already available. But when one carefully evaluates the materials, he discovers that a large percentage of the books are written for scholars in the field of marriage and the family, others are highly specialized, some are but collections of statistical information, still others are simply historical studies of the family and social change, but very few deal with the realities of two persons living together as man and wife in a very intimate interpersonal relationship. Few of the books are written in a language we can all understand and, therefore, we are unable to apply the concepts in our own relationships. *Everything You Need to Know to Stay Married and Like It* attempts to do just this. All extraneous discussion is omitted, all relevant and practical discussion is included.

The materials are theologically, psychologically, and sociologically sound in principle because they are based on solid research. However, the reader does not have to struggle through many long pages of charts, graphs, listings, and theoretical discussions before finding the important concepts.

The editor has attempted to eliminate all of the unnecessary "jargon" of the various disciplines so that the concepts are unmistakably clear and concise.

Couples preparing for marriage, newly married couples having problems in marital adjustment or seeking to enrich their marital experience, lay leaders of discussion groups both within the church and without, clergy, teachers, and others, will find the materials helpful for their own use, their unique needs and specific responsibilities. Obviously, no book in itself can be all things to all people, but the contents of this book can be a good beginning for everyone who reads it carefully.

The underlying theme of this book is that human relationships in marriage and family living are part of "continuing creation." Each person helps the other person to "become" a more complete person and by so doing he becomes a more complete person himself according to the potential God has ordained His human creation to attain. Each phase of the human life cycle can contribute in some way toward the fulfillment of persons if we are consciously aware of the process and utilize it to build persons. Each of the chapters is an attempt to help us to reach a higher level of relationship and potential rather than being content with the lower and less satisfying. Marriage and family living, and life in general, is what we make it, nothing more and nothing less. Few of us reach the potential possible. *Everything You Need to Know to Stay Married and Like It* is a book intended to help every couple create the best for each other and, therefore, have a happy and satisfying marriage. It is possible! Just try it! Do something about your life and marriage!

BENNARD WIESE
Editor and Author

Chapter 1

Marriage Is Real

THE MARRIAGE CEREMONY marks a definite step in the process of a mutual commitment of two people to each other. In it they face marriage as a real vocation that involves two real people in a real situation. Theoretically, the time of testing, maneuvering, and of insecurity has ended and the time of mutuality, commonality, and emotional security has begun. However, this process does not just happen, but it extends over a long period of time, during which the couple must learn by experience as they take specific roles and assume definite functions.

By its very nature, marriage is a task for two persons. It should be viewed as always being in the process of "becoming." Moment by moment the marriage partners prove whether their marriage is, at that particular point in time, a success or a failure. Individuals can, by really trying, order their lives so that the lives of both people can benefit and thereby create a climate in which love may grow stronger as each day passes. This attitude requires a basic faith in oneself as well as in one's partner. The point is clear: perseverance is necessary to make marriage a beautiful, satisfying, and mutually enriching experience.

Each married couple faces the need to make dual adjustments as they begin life together. In general, these needs are: First, how to deal constructively with the external pressures from culture, the insecurities resulting from war, inflation, recession, etc., which sometimes spoil even the best-made rational plans. (Furthermore, how can they stay married in an age when so many voices, rarely in harmony, are eager to give them "good" advice? Often unsolicited, eager advice comes from the family, the church, the state, science, social reformers and utopian dreamers.) Secondly, the couple faces internal adjustments as they seek to bring together two very unique personalities. Each person brings to marriage many pre-determined needs and expectations which may be quite different in degree or kind. This chapter and the following will deal with those areas crucial to adjustment as affected by both the external and internal pressures and expectations bearing on marriage. Greater emphasis will be placed on the internal factors as the authors believe these to be the most significant and of the greatest potential help for the reader.

The success of a marriage depends greatly on the materials going into it. There is hope for those who have chosen unwisely; however, this requires continuous, conscious, deliberate cooperation. Since the patterns of the early years of marriage become the settled habit of the later years, it will be helpful to turn to several of the factors which affect early successful adjustment.

Our culture has provided us with several myths surrounding marriage. These myths result in a great many false, phony feelings. One of the important myths is the "romantic myth" that is extremely significant during the pre-marriage, dating-courtship-engagement period. Basic to the myth is the idea that "our marriage is going to be different." It is going to be different because our partner will change after marriage and he will become a more lovable person.

Most studies of husband-wife grievances are amazingly similar and point clearly to the fact that the grievances are almost entirely personality faults and conflicts resulting from childhood conditioning and development.

A few examples to illustrate this are taken from L. M. Terman's *Psychological Factors in Marital Happiness* (McGraw Hill Book Co., 1938, p. 99). This order of marital grievances according to their seriousness was given by 792 husbands and 792 wives. Husbands listed the following against their wives: nagging, lack of affection, selfishness, inconsiderateness, complains too much, slovenly in appearance, and is quick-tempered. Included in the complaints of the wives were: selfishness, inconsideration, lack of success, untruthfulness, complains too much, lack of affection and failure to talk things over. Almost all the balance of the listings were also basic personality characteristics.

The most important things going into marriage then are individual attitudes, preferences, aversions, habit patterns, emotional response patterns, and basic temperament, which give or deny to one the aptitude of compatibility or adjustability. The marriage ceremony does not change these factors, even in a small way. Consequently, it is necessary to face the basic issue that for marriage to be successful, both partners must be willing to accept an attitude which includes the idea that "our marriage will be different because I will change, because I will make it different" – that our marriage is what we make it, and that our marriage is very real. Such an attitude helps overcome some basic feelings which lead to internal power struggles. If one's partner is forced to make all the changes, he may feel that his adaptations and adjustments required more sacrifice, that he is being twisted and distorted and that it hurts, and that he cannot be himself, and, therefore, he is forced to play a game and experiences a sense of phoniness and unreality. A person who is willing to change, to make a success of marriage, does not view change as a threat to his security and consequently he becomes a more adaptable person.

A second silly myth about marriage is the "myth of compatibility." This myth includes the idea that the couple just loves doing everything together because they are so much alike; their interests are almost exactly the same. It is enlightening to test out this "myth of compatibility" in a down-to-earth way. The married couple soon finds out some interesting things about each other which may be rather startling at first. The husband probably first discovers that his wife can't cook and maybe he has told her about this a time or two; or she can't keep house like his mother kept house; and likely he discovers she has some of the strangest relatives with whom a man ever became associated; and she has many quite disgusting habits he didn't recognize when they were single; and finally, she at times is inclined to be very unresponsive, something of a "cold potato."

The wife may soon also learn a good deal about the man she married. One of the primary things many women discover is that the male ego of which she was so proud during the dating days can drive her just "a little nuts." This great big hero she married is still in many ways an immature little boy; he too has many disgusting habits and the most unusual relatives she ever could imagine; and at times he is inclined to be something of a sex fiend. The marriage counselor recognizes the above to be common complaints from married people from all walks of life. They differ only in degree.

The real marriage experiences couples are involved in are often far different from the "romance type" they see in the mass media. These emphasize marriage as being totally and completely compatible. A false sense of mutuality and togetherness is built by emphasizing the desire of both to do the same things at the same time; a picture is presented of two people who just love spending all their lives together in happy bliss, always agreeing with each other.

What is the truth about compatibility? Couples entering marriage are totally different people – and they should be. They are not carbon copies of one another. The husband complements his wife, she complements him, and this is what can make marriage work. No one is entirely compatible, nor should they be. If a couple were totally compatible, they wouldn't or couldn't stay married – they would die of boredom in just a few years! Two very different people marry; they somehow need to learn to love each other, to recognize their similarities and build on these; but they also need to accept their differences and adjust. Couples need to recognize the fact that the specific differences are not really threatening to them, but rather it is what they do about their differences, and how they react to these differences, that is crucial. Too often, differences which potentially can enrich both the individual and the marriage, become the tension points which prevent the couple from finding success, mutual fulfillment, and happiness in marriage.

Another myth about marriage is that it automatically brings happiness. The search for happiness is often a motivation for marriage and when it does not come, disillusionment and despair often result. Too much emphasis today is placed upon happiness. The almost obsessive search for happiness as an end in itself often limits one's efforts to build into life those qualities which give lasting meaning and satisfaction to living. Successful marriage does bring happiness — a happiness which is more than just a good feeling. However, happiness can be the result of and not the reason for a successful marriage. Successful marriage is a growth process during which new understandings and new adjustments continue to be necessary at each stage of life. Life is never static; it is always dynamic. Happiness in marriage is built continuously and enhanced by several attitudes held by the couple. One of the important elements in the pattern of successful marriage is the commitment of the partners to a permanent union. Successful, happy marriages are just not possible if people go into the marriage experience with reservations, with time limits.

A second important attitude necessary for building a happy marriage is the commitment of both to a "will to succeed." When couples repeat the vows: "I take thee, ————, for better, for worse, for richer, for poorer, in sickness and in health until death," they are contracting for a lifetime of cooperation in all areas of living. Successful cooperation is not possible when limitations are set upon it. The seemingly crucial factor is the willingness or unwillingness to work at building a mutually satisfying relationship. The "will to succeed" is a significant factor, helping to overcome the negative meaning of differences. It is helpful to note that this attitude will not eliminate differences, but it will help to overcome them, help to work them out adequately and satisfactorily.

Total compatibility is a myth. Some lack of compatibility is found in every family and it is experienced all day long. Therefore, it becomes imperative that we go one step further in attempting to find and describe just what makes it possible for persons to experience the potential God has ordained men and women to achieve in the marriage relationship.

Is there one essential component of any successful marriage? The most essential component is the need for the development of a "mature married love" that makes it possible for a couple to live together over a long period of time. Compatibility is a myth; companionship we grow into; but love we must have and it must be a very deep love. What is love? Is it the deep, emotional, warm feeling that we like to think about; that we read about in the romance magzine; or is it something more than this? It is all this, but there is much more to it.

As we search for a definition of "mature love" we need to take a look at how love grows in marriage. We have two very different people entering marriage. Somehow they have to learn to love each other; somehow they have to achieve enjoyment, fulfillment, and happiness. How is this accomplished? There are no magic formulas, no panaceas, no easy outs. It takes a long time, and couples need to give it enough time to develop. (The author's concept of love is essentially based on 1 Corinthians 13. A valuable experience for the reader would be to use the *Good News for Modern Man* version and substitute his name whenever the word *love* is used.)

Probably every marriage goes through five distinct phases in the process of building mature married love. If real adult relationships are achieved they will have been achieved in a progression similar to the following process: a dream world stage; the time of disillusionment; the time of misery; the time of awakening; and the time of love. The reader should be aware that the growth of love in marriage does not always follow such routine patterns; yet the five stages apparently are fairly accurate generalizations that can be used for careful analysis of the subject of "mature adult married love."

The first stage, the "dream world stage," is a time when almost everything is possible, and almost everything is good, at least everything is going to be good tomorrow, or we will resolve the differences in the very near future. Life is a simple thing. My partner isn't just the way I want her, but tomorrow I will change her. The idea of change prevails during the "dream world stage" and is so common because it is a cultural inheritance continuing from the dating period. Couples are sure they will change because they "love each other so much."

Furthermore, they are not much concerned because each is sure that the other person is going to change and that this will solve all their problems. There are many frustrations, of course; new knowledge is gained about the other; differences are recognized; small quarrels with "kiss and make up" solutions are prevalent. Sex adjustment leaves a lot to be desired, but this will straighten out soon, as soon as the "other person changes." It is difficult for many persons, when they first become involved in this new, intimate relationship, to be objective enough to recognize that marriage, like any other interpersonal relationship, requires cooperation, emotional support, acceptance, mutual exchange, and a movement away from self-centeredness.

The "honeymoon idea" of the first months of marriage is probably one of the greatest myths in American marriage. Not always is there present this "good over all" feeling, this "wonderful, romantic love affair" for several weeks or months. In a honeymoon one encounters all kinds of "real" situations and some honeymoons are probably disasters, if the truth were known. Many persons during this stage discover that marriage is not an escape from reality and personal problems, but a continuation of life, albeit under new circumstances, with new problems and new responsibilities that are usually greater. These require a mutual meeting of personalities in a total relationship. Still there comes through this hope, this belief that tomorrow everything will be okay.

Every marriage moves from the "dream world stage" into the "time of disillusionment." This is a "real," necessary time through which most couples need to travel. It is a time of waking up and looking at marriage more realistically, seeing it as it "really is." The honeymoon is over. Tensions start to arise in the home; quite a few are sexual tensions, a number of which may not be so recognized, or may be directly related to other interpersonal tensions. Several of the more common sexual tensions would include premature ejaculation on the part of the male, the fear of pregnancy (or pregnancy itself), or perhaps a new baby or even two babies by this time. It becomes difficult to face up to the reasons for the tensions and so naturally each partner blames the other for the problem. As a consequence, various reactions and responses become evident. The wife may turn quite aggressive as she looks for love she feels she is not receiving. If she doesn't feel loved, she will shut out the husband during the time of disillusionment.

Because of tensions, communication gets tougher and tougher. Neither is willing to take the initiative in any discussion, nor is he willing to listen, to be honest, or open. Rather, both tend to become defensive, looking for scapegoats. Reactions become rigid and inflexible and they are inclined to personalize every difference and disagreement. A man may feel that there is no use arguing with these "stupid women." They just don't think straight. A woman often comes to the realization that her man perceives things in an entirely different way than she does and she may feel it is hopeless to try to communicate with him.

During the "time of disillusionment," there is often a real feeling of not being loved. There seem to be doubts because the couple has not yet developed empathy or adequate understanding of the needs and responses of the other person. They are sure of their own needs, responses, and love, but not yet sure of their partner's. There may be a feeling that they made a mistake, that some other marital choice might have been better, and that this would have eliminated the present problems. One of the tragedies of this period of emotional behavior is that of "retreatism." Rather than making a frontal attack on the problems, couples often fight for days and sulk for days, and no progress is made. The "time of disillusionment" is a very important period because it requires that the couple face up to the fact that they are married to real people and this presents to the couple in a conflict-tension confrontation the need to develop ways of reducing their points of disagreement, which is imperative in their movement toward "mature married love."

It would be great if at this point one could say that the couple would pass into something better. However, in most instances, they pass into a still deeper and worse phase which is called the "time of misery." In the United States today, one marriage out of four is broken by divorce, still others by desertion and others remain structurally intact, but emotionally and functionally broken (ratio of divorces to marriages, U.S. Bureau of the Census, 1967). These startling facts are a result of the inability of couples to work their way through this crucial stage. Some couples make a decision to get a divorce, others simply desert, but many continue to live out their married lives in the "time of misery." This is a miserable state, and one outstanding characteristic of this stage is the absence of hope in the minds of the spouses.

Everything seems to be going wrong. There are constant tensions in the home. An obvious doubt arises: "Why are we staying together under these circumstances?" Communication, except on the very trivial level of the mundane and superficial needs, is dead. The air in the home is electric and almost any response will result in an argument.

During the "time of misery" sex is dead. It is a no-love, duty situation and in many homes doesn't even exist. Some couples during this time have had no sexual intercourse for a year or more. Sometimes the progression moves from twin beds to different sleeping rooms if the "time of misery" goes on too long. Sex often is experienced on a "reward-punishment" basis during this stage with some very negative consequences. The man still feels he needs sex and he wishes he could do something else about it, but he doesn't know what to do. He tries to establish some sort of relationship with his wife. This "duty" reward or punishment kind of sex is a horrible thing. Most couples experience this sometime during their married life and it goes something like this. The woman resigns herself to cooperate because she's a good Christian or something of the kind and she feels "Oh boy, it's Tuesday night again, so go ahead, hurry, I've got other things to do." Or another situation might be: the day went fairly well, he took her out for dinner, so he deserves a little sex tonight. The tragedy is that their sex needs are real but they are frustrated and they become increasingly insecure in their sexual relationships with each other.

Too often the man, whom our culture has indoctrinated to solve his own problems, resolves that the only solution is to straighten out the "old lady." The woman is likely to confide in her mother or friends who really didn't think much of her husband to begin with. Consequently, there is no real attempt to move back together because they don't honestly believe it will be of any use. As they seek proof of love, they are feeling terribly alone, unloved, and sorry for themselves.

A rather clear picture is presented by the couple during this "time of misery." Expressed visually we see a picture of two people, the wife standing at one side of the room, the husband at the other side, both saying to each other. "I will love you when you love me." Neither is willing to move from this position and the marriage remains in the miserable stage. Unfortunately, this period lasts in some marriages all of the couple's lives. Neither one is able to accept responsibility for his own failures, but blames the other, and scapegoats by projecting his weaknesses on the other. Neither is able to look at himself with honesty and objectivity, or accept the present and work toward a mutually satisfying future. Neither is as yet other-centered, but is basically ego-centric. Both tend to take offense easily at what they interpret as slights and all interrelationships become excessively personalized. The "time of misery," therefore, lasts until someone, hopefully both, says, "We have to do something about this." From the "time of misery" the couple moves into a better time, the "time of awakening."

How does the couple move from a "time of misery" to a "time of awakening"? Basically, the couple moves there by facing marriage as a practical, down-to-earth experience that they have to build. After spending a great deal of time trying to change their partner, they take a look at themselves and say, "If this is going to be a better marriage, I'm going to have to work to make it better." This is where real love essentially begins in marriage. The couple entered marriage with a strong, romantic attraction, respect for each other; in other words, there was a nucleus of genuine love, but it was not mature. Since mature love has to begin in a creation of mature love in the home by the couple themselves, the couple begins to realize that they have been miserable for so long they finally are compelled to say: "Nuts, this has to stop." Someone makes a decision that he is going to make this work and then there is the discovery that it really isn't so hard to do because one who has lived through the time of misery knows exactly what it's going to take to make it work. Why does one know this? Simply because they have told each other many times what it's going to take to make it work, sometimes at the top of their voices with the neighbors listening, and sometimes through stubborn silences.

So someone sets out to make it work. Instead of staring at each other coldly from opposite sides of a room, someone says, "I love you." Quite obviously, after a long period of misery, little immediate response will be evident. Therefore, persistence in saying "I love you" is required. The new energy, ambition, and interest in life that this move engenders, accompanied by willingness to face reality and tackle problems realistically, brings response. Someone says, "Darling, let's get together. Let's make this work because I really do love you." This is a deliberate act of will which may certainly include a return to prayer to ask God's help as well as a change in attitude, realistic this time. Instead of a straightening-out-one's-partner routine, it becomes "God help us" to make our marriage what it is potentially capable of becoming (Mark 11:24-26; James 5:16).

Change does not come about immediately. The one who makes the first move may expect to be rejected at first. For example, if the man makes the first move, the woman may feel, "Oh boy, he's trying to make out with me again." We read in First Corinthians 13, that "love never fails." Therefore, if one persists something will begin to happen, because when one gives love, love is returned. Love freely given is an irresistible force. It does work. The marital relationship begins to change as the partners attempt to concentrate on making possible the happiness of the other person instead of making excessive demands on each other. There are still bad times. There are ups and downs, but the big difference now is that there is hope which brings increased self-confidence, trust, and security. If the couple persists, they can move into a very beautiful time called the "time of love." The couple are no longer concerned about remodeling each other but they love each other for what they are, faults and all.

The "time of love" is a beautiful phase of marriage, but a very strange one. It's beautiful, but it is real. It's not like it was in the romance magazines; the couple is not compatible even here. Everything isn't perfect, but it's a real time. The most significant thing that has happened is that the couple has accepted one another most of the time the way he or she is. Acceptance of the other person is basic. It is almost always the first step in creating a relationship. Acceptance makes possible a love with no prerequisites. Once the couple has learned acceptance, each of the other as he is, they can more easily say to each other the six hardest words in the English language, "I was wrong – I am sorry." Once they have learned to express these words they will find it much more possible to "forgive and forget." This requires concentrated effort by the couple so that they do not fall into the trap of requiring the other to prove his worthiness, or of expressing, "I will love you only when you love me or are worthy of my love." (For love without prerequisites, see First John 4:19 and Romans 5:8.)

The "time of love" restores reality, down-to-earth, honest communication. Trust has been restored, growth toward mature married love is possible. What happens during the time of love? The following statements are only descriptive and analogous, but are useful for improving our understanding. The woman wakes up in the morning and looks at her husband sleeping beside her and she says, "I love you, you great big beautiful hunk of man." As he's lying there, he's snoring a little. The first few years she had thought many times about sticking a clothespin on his nose to stop him from snoring and she was determined that she was going to change him. He still has other irritating habits. He doesn't call her during the day. He doesn't tell her he loves her very often, and he kind of ignores her completely at times. But still she has this feeling of goodness and warmth and love. Why? Because she has accepted him.

The man wakes up in the morning and looks at his sleeping wife. She is snoring a little and a few years ago one of the things that irritated him most about his wife was that she snored a little. And he looks at her and he says: "Man, I love you, you wonderful girl." And then, all of a sudden the thought hits him. *Why? She still snores, she doesn't cook so well, she is kind of sloppy about housekeeping, she doesn't do the dishes right after dinner. In other words she hasn't changed very much. I was certain she had to change. But I love her and I want her the way she is.*

During the "time of love" sex becomes a beautiful, mutual experience. Whereas it formerly was a thing they fought about, now sex brings them together, the man's desires are in complete harmony with his wife's desires and when she doesn't want to, he doesn't want to. Both begin to desire what the other person wants and needs. An interesting consequence is an almost immediate subsiding of want on the part of both. Neither needs to prove anything, ego strengths are enhanced, supportive relationships are strengthened, a beautiful, total, mutual relationship is established.

An awareness of the five phases of married life are necessary for one to recognize that marriage is for real and that all couples go through the same kind of searching process on their way to building mutual love. A knowledge about the phases helps one to overcome a basic "hang-up," especially found among young couples, that their problems are their own and their solutions are their own, consequently, they become looped into an almost irresolvable situation and become submerged in their own problems.

What then is this thing called love? It is not possible to define it. The most significant thing for anyone to recognize is that love never comes to us full-grown and mature. The only kind of love one gets out of marriage is the one we are responsible for because we have built it.

For Summary and Review

1. What do you think about the statement: "Individuals can, by really trying, order their lives so that the lives of both people can benefit and thereby create a climate in which love may grow stronger as each day passes"?
2. Discuss the statement: "Success of a marriage depends greatly on the materials going into it." What are the implications which need consideration?
3. What insights into marriage can be gained by studying carefully Terman's rank order of marital grievances?
4. Of what importance is the attitude: "Our marriage is going to be different because I will change"?
5. Do you agree with the statement that "compatibility" is a myth? Why? Why not? Explain your answer.

6. Is the person's search for happiness a valid reason for getting married? Why? Why not? Explain.
7. Evaluate the "five stages" of marriage carefully. Are they valid? What important concepts do you feel are identified by using this analysis of maturing married love?
8. Why is "acceptance" of the other person basic in building love in marriage?
9. To what extent is the person responsible for building love in the home? How does your answer compare with the "romantic concept" of love?
10. Some people point out that marriage should be a trial situation. If it doesn't work out, then we would be free to seek another relationship. What do you think of this approach? Explain fully!
11. If you were writing this chapter, what would you have included that is not now included? List the specific strengths and/or weaknesses as you see them.

Chapter 2

A Formula for Building Love in the Home

WHAT IS A FORMULA? A dictionary definition declares that it is "an exact or prescribed method or form for doing something; an established rule." We are constantly exposed to many formulas, some concrete and meaningful, others vague and meaningless, others extremely oversimplified such as "the family that prays together stays together" and "the family that plays together stays together." We are confronted with all kinds of simple little plans that are supposed to solve all of our problems in every human relationship.

Can a formula be applied for building love in the home? Obviously one specific formula cannot be used for building love in marriage because every couple is entirely different from every other couple. Each couple has to figure out their own particular method for making their marriage grow. However, there seemingly is a basic routine that almost all people who finally arrive at a satisfactory, happy marriage follow. For purposes of analysis, this basic routine will be called a formula in this chapter. It is not an easy formula, it's a tough one, because it requires a good deal of effort and change on the part of both partners.

The basic formula is deceptively simple. It begins with good communication, plus hard work, plus for Christians, prayer. Very simple: Communicate—Work—Pray=Mature Love. We need to recognize that making this simple formula work is an enriching but difficult task for the couple.

Communication is a favorite process today for ailing human relationships. We are told that more communication would be a solution to most problems (personal to international). Young couples about to be married are convinced by ministers, counselors and teachers, reinforced by articles in the news media, that their marriages will never break up "because we can talk to each other and because we can discuss our problems together." The assumption behind these beliefs is that many, if not all, problems exist because people do not communicate and therefore do not understand one another. It should be made quite clear at this juncture that it is not the sheer volume or accuracy of communication which is crucial. The communication which is part of the formula does not refer to superficial communication, but rather the communication, talking and thinking, needs to be about things that really matter in one's marriage. Probably selective communication is the key to success as there are some thoughts, desires, and attitudes which may be destructive, and bring adverse reaction, when communicated. "Good" communication can be distinguished from just everyday talking together. Many couples go through their entire lives without ever really establishing good communication between one another. There is a lot of talk, but it's about the weather, the World Series, the favorite TV show, the latest dress styles – really never about things of importance to them as a couple. They do not really sit down and talk together about things that really matter to them and therefore, one of the basic characteristics of "good" communication is missing.

For purposes of focusing attention on specific areas of communication, we will divide communication into several separate areas. The most important part of communication is called "communication with self." The second significant and necessary area of communication is "communication with each other." A final consideration of communication deals with "communication with God." Later chapters will identify and discuss other important characteristics of "good" communication as they relate to the enrichment of the "marriage experience."

What is meant by communication with self? The most important aspect of this area of communication is the attempt to find answers to three significant questions: Who am I? What do I want to become? How do I get there?

Marriage is a maturing union of two maturing individuals. Most newlyweds, even those who felt they knew themselves and each other well before marriage, suddenly find themselves facing problems and adjustments different from anything they had imagined and greater in significance. The couple soon discover that living as married people is different from any previous experience they had shared. As basic personality traits, values, and habits become expressed overtly in marriage, the newly married couple suddenly come to an awareness that they are not at all "just alike" and that they do not completely agree on everything, as they were so sure they would during their dating years. As they face the necessary adjustments and adaptations inherent in married life, there is need for answers to the questions which arise concerning themselves, their partner, and their marriage. The couple must move from immaturity to maturity in their relationship. Therefore, if the spouses as individuals do not grow up, the marriage can never mature. Communication with self begins with a realistic, hard look at oneself and is followed by a constant analysis, a constant questioning, as one seeks to know oneself. Only then can one start to grow up and try to make oneself into what he feels he needs and wants to be. Furthermore, only then can communication with one's partner become constructive and uplifting. Obviously there is some overlapping which occurs in the specific area of communication we have identified, for to understand himself, man needs to be understood by another, and to be understood by another he needs to understand the other person.

Honesty in communication with self is difficult to maintain. We do like to kid ourselves; we do like to compare our own characteristics with others to boost our own ego or reinforce our own negative self-concepts. One of the specific ways that we use to kid ourselves is by what the psychologists call "projection." "Projection" is the unconscious process of attributing one's own feelings and attitudes to others. It is often used as a defense against guilt or feelings of inferiority by blaming other people for our own behavior and the consequence of this behavior. Projection is a psychological mechanism which is very commonly experienced. Extremes could be viewed as indicative of immaturity. Kids project almost all the time, adults in varying degrees; all this is directly related to their maturity.

It will be helpful to look at several examples of projection to see specifically how it works and how it prevents us from facing differences squarely in life and, therefore, prevents the development of adequate communication which leads to mature married love.

A young boy, your son, eight or nine years of age, is playing ball in a vacant lot next door. Several other boys are also there and they are playing catch with a hardball. Perhaps your youngster misses a swiftly thrown ball and it goes through one of your windows. Your response likely will be to rise up in righteous wrath and you will demand to know who it was who perpetrated this act. You will demand to know who is responsible for this ball coming through the window. So what does your little boy say? Probably he will be inclined to say, "It's Johnny's fault, daddy. He threw the ball. I didn't miss the ball, Johnny threw it, it is his fault." Your son projected all the blame on someone else and assumed no responsibility for his own behavior. The interesting thing is that we expect this kind of behavior from children. We think of it as a childish kind of behavior. But is it really? Don't adults often respond in the same way?

If we consider for a moment the response of an alcoholic who goes off and gets himself royally "sopped" about two nights a week and responds to the question, Why do you drink so much? In all seriousness he may say, "You'd drink too, if you were married to the old biddy I'm married to." He spent most of his free time at the local bar; he didn't come home some nights; still it was her fault that he drank. Again, the above is an example of a failure to be a responsible, self-accepting person. It is easier to say someone else is at fault than to get hold of and change ourselves.

How would you respond, for example, if you were just leisurely driving down a street, and suddenly, you almost ran into a guy at an intersection because you didn't stop? Would you have an automatic built-in response? Would you look squarely at the other guy and say to him, "Why don't you look where you're going? It's your fault, not mine"?

A final example of projection can be found in the following illustration. A woman comes into a marriage counseling office and sits down across from the counselor. One of the facts that keeps cropping up as the counselor seeks to get a picture of this marriage is that she is a terrible housekeeper. Finally, the counselor says to her. "Well, if you are so worried about this, why don't you pick up the house once in a while?" And she replies, "If you were married to a character who didn't appreciate anything you do, you wouldn't clean the house either. It's his fault, not mine." The interesting fact is that it's her house that is a mess. She is the one who has to live in it and face the mess every day. But it is his fault that he does not appreciate her. Projection, the constant blaming of each other, needs to be brought from the unconscious to the conscious level so that self-development and maturity will be possible. The basic difference then between a mature adult and a child is that the adult accepts responsibility for his or her acts, no matter how stupid they may have been. "I did it"; "It's my act, I'm responsible for it and I'll take responsibility for it myself."

Communication with our partner is a second part of our formula. The concepts will only be introduced in this chapter and much more will follow throughout this book. Most spouses need to learn to do two basic things. One is to be honest, to quit pretending, to quit hiding, to quit being the big strong men, to quit being extremely feminine women and all kinds of other facades and learn to tell your partner who you are. Secondly, most persons need to learn to listen to their spouses when they want to tell them who they are.

Listening becomes easier when the communication between husband and wife is based on self-respect and respect for one's mate. Each spouse must also learn to proceed on the fundamental conviction that nothing is so important as to warrant the violation of integrity in marriage – his own or his mates. Therefore, communication needs to be undertaken with the conviction that the persons in marriage are the most important. Both spouses must be motivated to both talk and listen; it cannot be one-sided. Listening must become an active art as one (receiver) learns how to give complete attention to the one who is talking (sender). Another requirement (which takes time) is for each to be conscious of the other's vocabulary which contains the meanings, the emotions, and the responses of the person (content or message). There is a need to be aware of personal references, personalization, complexes, sensitivities, fears, values, biases, and resistances which are present during attempts at communication. Basically then, if a spouse has something that he feels he needs to tell, the other needs to listen, to attempt to discover what he is trying to say. Consequently, communication is a first part of our formula, work is the second. There is no secret formula, no short cut, no quick and easy way; it must be worked out.

Hard work and cooperation are a tremendously important part of our formula because marriage is a union of two maturing persons. It seldom begins that way. One of the most startling discoveries the couple makes is that the man is really married to a little girl and the woman is married to a little boy. These are tough discoveries to make. The differences and behaviors (whether superficial habits such as failing to put the cap on the tooth paste container, or in deeper attitudes such as the meaning of money) cannot be submerged for long. The imaginative expectations and dreams of the wedding day must give way to a willing recognition that all of us are just imperfect, immature human beings. Because of this fact, in some way the man has to help the woman grow up into a woman and the woman has to help her guy mature into a responsible man. This takes work, a conscious, deliberate effort, because often the persons bring such high expectations and great fears into marriage. They sought and expected the other's unjustified approval, and each hoped to realize through the other what they never found in themselves. When this does not happen immediately, they feel crushed, angry, betrayed and defeated. Neither men nor women come ready made. "Ladies, if you want a man, you have to build one; and men if you want a woman, you have to build one." This is a building process. We have to build men and women and the best place to do this is at home.

It is not so difficult as one might think, although it may seem tough at times. Basically two techniques are involved – love and communication. In the home we have the two best psychiatrists possible because of their love, care and concern for each other; they have a great deal of vested and invested interest in the marriage. Every time one works to create a better spouse, one has more fun, more enjoyment, and more love. Because all of us need love, this relationship is important to us.

As part of this process, many of us have to learn to permit our partner to be what he should be, and what he wants to be. We are created as irreplaceable individuals, different from any who have gone before or who will appear again. Often this can be a frightening, threatening thought to insecure people who have not realized that each person is a talented individual with unique worth. Too many differences paralyze them and lead to disagreements. All this is viewed as a competitive fight for survival, or it is considered dangerous. When we discussed the dream world stage in Chapter 1, we discussed the unfortunate fact that many persons spend all kinds of time trying to change each other and remodeling each other according to predetermined concepts of what a "good" spouse should be.

The tremendous amount of time that is wasted in marriage trying to change partners calls for attention to a very important characteristic of our temperament we will call "conflict with authority." It is not something new, it is universal and each person has a definite conflict with authority. How do you react, for example, when someone tells you: "This must be done! This is what you must do! This is the way it must be done! You have to! You must!"? Is your reaction one of acceptance, or are you likely to respond either verbally in no uncertain terms: "Like fun I do," or covertly with seething antagonism and resentment? Don't we, realistically, usually respond, "We don't have to do anything of the kind"? A built-in conflict with authority is something we all have. Most of us like to be led to a certain extent, we like authority to a certain extent, but we like reasonable authority consistently. If we recognize the built-in conflict with authority, it becomes much clearer to us that remodeling or forced change imposed on our spouse can be very destructive. After long patterning, the consequences could be either an over-dependent mate or a domineering mate, both lacking self-esteem. Two contradictory meanings could also be found, "I am nothing; I will live for you," and also, "I am nothing; therefore you must live for me completely." The only constructive way to change is through love (Romans 13:10; 1 John 4:18). No one can force a woman to change her habits; no one can force a man to change his habits. Men often believe they can change women; after all they are bigger, wider, heavier, and if they shout loud enough, wave a big club or use threats, the little lady will do the dishes immediately after dinner. Coercion, of course, can be used to intimidate and change overt expressions of behavior for a short time, but something happens when we do this. Facetiously, we can envision her salting the soup all too liberally the next time she makes soup. Or we can picture her in bed at night, daring the man to try to make love to her. What is this but an example of conflict of authority?

Why then do persons change in marriage? They change because they love, and if love is not received, one will not basically change. This is what acceptance is all about. It is a clear recognition that I cannot change my partner; that he or she is what he is and the only thing that will change this person is love. Therefore, it is necessary to accept him or her as he or she is. There is only one way change really occurs, and this is through love, through care, and through concern. We change because we want to change; this is the thing that will make our marriage better. There will be more love because I have made a change. It would be helpful for each of us to accept the other person and permit the other person to be, and then we could begin admiring what the other person totally is.

What is the sense of trying to change people anyway? Doesn't one basically marry a certain kind of individual because one needs that kind of a person? Each person has gaps or holes in his personality which can be bridged or filled by his mate's personality. One spouse may be careless with money and so that kind of person is married to one who is as close and frugal as they come. She is needed for this reason and in turn she needs her husband for many reasons. Therefore, what's the sense to try to change her into a carbon copy of oneself, when she is needed as the kind of person she is? For marriage to reach its highest potential people must be complementary. Both consciously and unconsciously we marry individuals because we need individuals of this particular kind. This is what marriage really is all about; that is, it is an attempt to complete individual personalities.

Each individual wants to be loved for himself or herself, faults and all. Each also needs to develop understanding of the other spouse and self-understanding. Both come about as a result of good communication. We face another problem at this point in our understanding. Husbands and wives seem to have one thing in common; they all believe they are mind readers and when there is a communication breakdown in the home, essentially this is what is happening. The husband thinks he knows what his wife is thinking and he really does not understand at all; and the wife thinks she understands what her husband is thinking while realistically, she does not know what he is thinking at all. This is one of the most common sources of communication difficulty in a marriage relationship! the assumption by the spouses that they know what the other means or feels by a certain action, word, or gesture. Expression and tone of voice result in a real tendency to project one's own observations or feelings onto the spouse. "I know how you feel."

Important in solving this dilemma is the necessity of talking together and developing an art of asking for explanation, repetition, and clarification to track down specifics instead of generalizations. It is also necessary to recognize that logic has little to do with the habits people develop. Feelings, rational or irrational, are the motives for human actions – not logic. Tolerance, empathy, sympathy, and understanding is called for here and not condemnation for illogical inconsistency. Furthermore, some communication breaks down over a false principle of "right" or "wrong." Usually there is no absolute right or wrong side in marital disagreements, just different sides or understandings. Differences in marital conflict can be understood, diminished, compromised, and sometimes even eliminated. However, this cannot happen unless one stops looking for "the right" and "the wrong."

Married couples must become aware of the fact that absolutes are serious blocks to marital communication. When spouses try to understand the degrees of their differences rather than acting as judges who condemn and criticize, they will often find their differences much less in quantity and importance. Acceptance, communication, cooperation, and mutuality all become easier when couples begin to recognize the normality of this requirement for a successful marital relationship.

Finally, there is one more dimension to the formula which is of great significance in the "Christian" home. As James 5:16 states: "The effectual fervent prayer of a righteous man availeth much." Even those people who claim to be atheist usually claim to be broad-minded; therefore, those who reject the power of prayer in the lives of millions of people world wide belie their broad-mindedness. Prayer does change things, for God answers prayer – also in this that true praying assumes and works within the person praying an attitude which predisposes a response that will enhance the relationship. Prayer also changes people. One who prays soon discovers that "prayer does change things" (1 Thessalonians 5:17; Mark 11:24; Luke 18:1; James 5:16).

Most people need prayer because as human beings we are tremendously complicated beings. We have discussed understanding ourselves, finding ourselves, and evaluating or facing up to ourselves. One can never fully understand why he acts as he does. How then can one possibly understand another person who may be more complicated still? Or at least seems to be because he's a different person. To accomplish this difficult task to the highest degree possible one has a great need for God through prayer. In our Christian tradition this help has always been available, but most of us neglect to make use of it or do so very superficially because there is not always a clear recognition of God's place in every marriage.

How can one approach God in marriage more realistically through real prayer and real communication? Couples frequently are totally unrealistic in their prayers. Often they look for something that just doesn't happen to most people. They are looking for God to take over their partner and straighten him out, cure him of his bad habits, coerce him into being what they want their partner to be. The prayer often goes something like this: "Lord, make Charlie stop drinking." Is this not hypocrisy when we say to God, "You know, I'm good and he's bad, so fix him over, God, so I can live with him." Not only is such a statement or expectation hypocritical, it is also ridiculous. It is dictating to God and therefore it will not work. Prayer offered with this motivation does not fit into the context of the New Testament at all. It certainly does not fit into the context of humility and love as it is described in the Scriptures by God Himself (Luke 11: 1-4; Hebrews 11:6; James 4:6-8).

A Christian response to God includes a willingness to be patient in working out the various solutions. As we read in Ephesians 4:2, "with all lowliness, and meekness, with long-suffering, forbearing one another in love." J. B. Phillips translates this verse: "Accept life with humility and patience, making allowances for one another because you love one another." Humility means that one is committed to the reality that he is not always right and the idea that one is never all right in the complexity of personal differences. But most important is the fact that a humble person is a teachable person; he is capable of learning from and through his experience.

Real prayer and communication with God begins with humility and recognition of dependence on God: "God, human beings are complicated and I can't figure them out alone. Help me to understand. Help me to accept. Help me to move beyond the selfish, egotistical, presumptuous view that I hold about myself." So basically the need is to overcome the concept found in the following verse of poetry (Roy W. Fairchild, *Christians in Families,* p. 169): "In matters controversial my perception is quite fine. I always see both points of view. The one that's wrong – and mine" (Author unknown).

Prayer can be meaningful if we only stop dictating to God and stop asking Him to put His stamp of approval on our own outline of the problem. We need to approach God with humility and say, "Lord, we're in trouble. Help us. Help us to realize what we can do to make this a better marriage" (Matthew 6:10; Psalm 16:11).

In this chapter we have identified and discussed three points that seem to be most significant in the development of a formula for building love in the home. The formula has been stated as involving "communication, work, and prayer." They are three very interrelated parts. For man to understand himself, he needs to be understood by others and to be understood by another he needs to understand the other. This is what communication is all about between husband

and wife, between parents and children. We need God's help in building good communication. Through prayer we find the help necessary to build ourselves and our partner. It is a very simple formula to state but not so easy to follow. If one is committed to all three parts it will work. Try it!

For Summary and Review

1. Why is "communication" placed in the first part of the formula for building love in the home? Do you agree with the discussion with respect to the importance of communication? Why? Why not?
2. Why is "honesty in communication with self" so difficult? How and why do we so often avoid communicating with ourselves?
3. Why are we sometimes afraid to communicate with our partner about issues that really matter?
4. Discuss: "Nothing is so important as to warrant the violation of *integrity* in marriage."
5. Discuss the second part of the formula which is work. How is work related to the statement: "Ladies if you want a man, you have to build one; and men if you want a woman, you have to build one"?
6. Discuss: "People don't change people; love changes people."
7. How real is the concept of "conflict with authority"? How does it affect marital growth and adjustment?
8. Why can prayer be such an important part of building love in the home? What meanings does prayer have for a marital relationship?
9. After considering the contents of Chapters 1 and 2, what is your present concept of mature married love? What relationship is there between our love at the time of marriage and the Biblical parable of the mustard seed (Matthew 13:31-32)?
10. What are the strengths and weaknesses of this chapter? Be specific in identifying ways it could be improved in content.

Chapter 3

Thinking About Talking

Communication is important in marriage. It is often said that when a couple have a marital problem that they should "talk it over." But because there is an unavoidable incompleteness of communication, discussion of the difference is not an automatic solution for marital problems. Much discussion can occur without much real communication taking place. Because of the incompleteness of communication, understanding is also incomplete. Too often each spouse believes that he or she is completely honest and is clearly stating and dealing with all of the pertinent facts. To a degree this may be true; however, interpretations of the facts may ultimately be the most important. Communication in the home needs to be consciously and deliberately built. The major emphasis of this chapter will be on how couples can learn to talk to each other about things that really matter.

Here is an illustration out of the experience of Urban Steinmetz while he was doing marriage counseling. It is effective because it can help us to focus our attention on several aspects of both good and bad communication. It is a true account, slightly abridged, about a couple referred to him by an attorney, late on a hot summer day, just prior to a two-week vacation planned by the counselor.

> So on this particular day, the couple came in. I was in a hurry, and I didn't know what to do with them because the next two weeks I couldn't see anybody. I was already overloaded with cases. So I called them into the office and gave

> them a quick talk on communications. You know, the old standard routine about who solves your problems, you do. Now, obviously you have a problem, go home and talk about it.
>
> Well, they walked out of the office and it was very funny the way they went out, if it hadn't been so sad. They didn't look to the left or the right. They didn't say a word. They didn't say anything to the secretary. They just stalked out of the office like two little kids. You know, like we all do when we are angry at each other. They crawled into the car, still not saying a word. They started for home, stopped for a six-pack of beer. The man went in and got it and came back to the car. She glared at him. I suppose because he maybe had picked up too many six-packs this week. They then went on home and there was still this dead, deep silence.
>
> They got home and she cooked the supper, put it on the table, they ate. Still no conversation. So finally, after supper, he went to the refrigerator and took out two bottles of beer and set one in front of her and one in front of himself. Then he leaned over to her and sort of pointed his finger under her nose. Then he said, "Now look, woman, that marriage counselor said we should talk. Now darn you, talk!"
>
> The surprising thing about this story is that it does have a happy ending. She did talk. For an hour and a half she talked about everything under the sun. She told him exactly how she felt, what she thought about him, about his disgusting habits, about his relatives, and she told him that he was about as romantic as a "glob of gook." And finally she began to cry. And when she started to cry, she said this beautiful thing. "I must be out of my mind. If I had any sense I'd leave you. I'd go through with the divorce. But, I guess I must love you, because I don't want to go through with it."

A lot of good communications are in this simple example. First, the man in the story listened. He listened and heard exactly what she was saying. Too often listening occurs without one actually hearing his spouse. One may appear to be attentive without really entering his spouse's life or thoughts at all. Too often only an impression of listening is given when in fact we are preoccupied with other pressing matters that are on our minds. There are other reasons why we don't listen and hear. Possibly we are preoccupied precisely to avoid the close involvement in another life that listening might bring. It could be that when our spouse becomes a little bit critical we become defensive because we feel threatened and we are afraid really to face ourselves. We are afraid to find out exactly what we are like and, therefore, we try to protect ourselves from a knowledge that we may be at fault and that we need to change. Many times the listener also engages in selective inattention so that he hears only those messages he desires to hear and he may also watch for mistakes in what the other person is saying, not to discover anything about himself, but to be able to get back at or attack the spouse with this mistake. Most poor listeners are more concerned about protecting themselves than in gaining understanding.

Intelligent learning-listening means that one listens with the idea: "Could this be me?" It can work beautifully in marriage because who knows more about you than the person to whom you are married? Who can describe you more accurately? Who can help you to be a better person than the person you have been living with?

Good listening helps develop empathy and understanding of the spouse. As one gets to know the other person a knowledge of what and when to speak is obtained and a balance between listening and talking is achieved. Furthermore, good listening makes one aware of the barriers in communication such as lack of confidence which is often the result of doubts, suspicion, moralizations, chastisements, castigation, apathy, lack of interest, and ego defenses. Trust and honesty can be restored to your communication and acceptance of the other person can become real and then one will not be so apt to shut off the communication before the meanings come through. Sharing of things which are important becomes a possibility and communication is continuous rather than sporadic, self-centered, and exploitative. Intelligent listening-learning helps one to understand oneself, who he is, and why he acts as he does. Likewise, it also helps one to understand the other as well as to be understood by the other. Even when we are tempted to complain, "He doesn't understand me" or "I can't understand her," we can be sure that we will never completely understand one another. However, we can consciously work toward sending clearer messages and becoming better listeners. We become persons through communication and through communication we confirm the other's existence. We cannot help but communicate. Even silence contains a message. We can find out a great deal by listening intelligently.

Secondly, the communication in the illustration was honest. The wife didn't spare any words but she laid it on the line. Her husband didn't have any romance in him at all that she could see. As is too often the case, it was this sort of approach: "Let's go to bed and make love, honey." "Honey" was a word that just happened to slip out at bedtime. So she told him exactly what she thought of this kind of an approach. This was good because it was honest and because he actually learned what kind of person he really was.

Most couples are not very honest with each other in marriage. Too often they play the game of "let's pretend." Let's pretend that our problems will go away by themselves. Let's pretend that we are better than we are. Let's not admit we have any feelings. All of these things are basically dishonest in that they do not face reality; nor do we as married couples want to face what we are as persons. It is much easier to pretend it is the wife's fault or the husband's fault and it becomes difficult to talk to each other about it because it might hurt. The courage to be real persons, to be real with each other, is a freedom persons can have in communication in the home. Honesty is one of the great dividends of life and it has an amazing effect on others around us because we no longer feel the need to project and find a scapegoat or brood about our circumstances. Courage to be honest enables one to speak the truth in love which will end the unnecessary pain and guilt placed upon ourselves. The expression of honest feelings can be positive evidence that the individual is secure enough to be himself, and that the couple themselves are secure, even though they continue to experience conflict and differences which are present in everyday living.

Thirdly, good communications in every home have to be about everything. There are social taboos about communicating or receiving certain kinds of information and the couple needs to be alert about the sensitivities and tolerances of each other. Nevertheless, communication needs to be about "everything in the book." We have to talk about money; we have to talk about sex; we have to talk about disciplining children; we have to talk about child-rearing practices; we have to talk about in-laws, etc., to name just a few for illustration (these seem to be difficult areas for many). We need to talk about all of the things important to this particular, unique marriage. How often is this an accomplished task? Most of the time we avoid this frontal confrontation. Why? One of the major reasons apparently is that soon after marriage differences of opinion and habit resulted in a quarrel and this was painful to them. The consequence was that from that time on they avoided particular aspects or content in their communication. Couples develop a method of problem solving and this becomes the settled habit. Too often they accept at face value the insidious "old-wives' tale" that is a real obstacle to communication — that "silence is golden." Other methods are resorted to such as: the wife always gives in, no decision is reached, the subject is closed, they break off in an angry exchange, or hopefully agreement is reached by a mutual give-and-take. A great tragedy occurs when the couple cannot, or does not try, to combine the inevitable differences that ultimately could arise into a workable, satisfying way of life.

To make it possible for both spouses to be open and complete in their communication, both must talk with love. Only with love can one work out the delicate balance that exists between oneself and the other and bring about a strength and security which makes it unnecessary to quarrel, fight, or flee (escape) from their differences. In our illustration, this woman was not very romantic either. She said: "I guess I don't have any sense, because if I did I would leave you." What an expression! But still this was tremendously important to the man because he really didn't think or believe she did love him. A closely related factor is that too often spouses tend to take each other for granted. The result is that they often find out that it is difficult to say to each other with meaning, "I love you." The man especially may find it difficult to show affection toward his wife because our culture teaches that this kind of display of emotions is "feminine" and therefore to be avoided.

Love words, such as honey, darling, dear, sweetheart, and other mutual expressions can and do have a tremendous amount of meaning, especially when communication is honest and complete. Too often, for some reason, we do not seem to think our partner needs to be told that we love him, but we would be quick to recognize that we ourselves need desperately these assurances. Don't all persons need to know that they are loved and can they find it out in any other way except as we tell each other once in awhile? It appears to be absolutely essential to every successful marriage for each to learn to say with meaning, "I care, I love you, I am concerned about you." If couples can learn to do this, they have overcome a damaging assumption that because we are married, "of one flesh and blood," and live together in the same home, that love and its expression are automatically included in the package. Love thrives on expression and response; so is it also with anger, irritation, and criticism which will soon destroy love. Love, consideration, and understanding rank high on the list of strengths of happily married couples. As each spouse expresses love for the other, attempts to concentrate on the other's happiness instead of his own, mutual self-fulfillment is possible.

Finally, the illustration points out another important concept. The couple had a real give-and-take battle before the evening was over. Possibly this is something that every couple needs occasionally in their marriage. A "good fight" or "creative conflict" once in awhile can serve a very important function in almost every home because it is often absolutely necessary to "clear the air"; and if there is no other way of doing it, it can be cleared with a "good fight" that settles something.

Disagreements are inevitable at many points in marriage and family living. Sometimes spouses become competitors as well as helpers and complements to one another. Rather than the isolation and alienation which accompanies conflict too often in the home, couples need to overcome the loneliness, to reduce the personal hurt, retaliation and recrimination. To accomplish this, differences must be brought out into the open so that good communication can be restored. Angry reactions are inevitable in a person's life, especially in the closeness and intimacy of family life, but the most important consideration is what one does with anger.

There are times in every home when tensions become so great that spouses just can't stand each other any longer. At this point no communication is possible because every response becomes a negative, destructive one. Perhaps, if this happens, the thing that will clear the air and end the tension will be a "good fight." It may even require the couple to fight it through, to talk it through, at the top of their voices. However, our culture has conditioned us not to fight. Nothing is so disturbing to parents, for example, as fighting among their children. What is the consequence of this conditioning? Jealousy, resentment, and hostility between brothers and sisters is a continuing theme in the world's literature. By overlooking the constructive features of some anger and quarreling, we are conditioned to look for outlets for our personal frustrations in some other way which leads to the failure to compromise, estrangement, unfriendliness, and helplessness. Everyone needs to find ways to express both love and aggression in some way. The destructive ways involve conflict, separation and silence; the constructive ways include conflict, conciliation and reconciliation. The former suggests that there is no problem so big that you cannot escape from it; the latter suggests that the only way to solve a problem is to face the issues squarely and that even extreme differences need not break one's love. This basically then explains the difference between a "bad" and a "good" fight.

It would be helpful for us to clarify the issues. Therefore, we will take a brief look at the kind of fights which are common with most couples. The reader will recognize quickly that these are destructive, "bad" fights. Preceding the actual fight, one finds a constant bickering; it never seems to end. Mom says a few quick words she thinks are especially for dad's benefit. He retaliates with a few well-chosen words he thinks will help her, you know, straighten her out. Of course he believes that he is really helping her and is not nagging at all. We become very expert in this kind of behavior after we have lived together for a long period of time in close intimacy. We have learned very perceptively just how to hurt the other the most with words. The unfortunate part of this "bad fight" is that at this juncture one of the spouses usually stops the fight. He quits. One of the partners says, "Oh, boy, if we go on with this, we're in trouble."

At this point all kinds of escapist behavior can be expected from either or both. For example, the wife begins to cry and she runs out of the room into the bedroom, slams the door, and says to herself: *There is no use in arguing with him, he is impossible*, and that ends the conversation. However, probably a better example, found in many homes, would be the man running away. He walks out, slams the door, says, "Oh, for heaven's sake, you impossible woman, its impossible trying to talk with you." Then he storms out of the house and sulks while he busies himself at some activity at home or away. Late that night he comes in and wakes up his wife, if she is sleeping, but probably only pretending, and says: "Honey, I really love you." The man may escape in many other ways. He may work late, spend time at the club with the guys, or busy himself with some hobby. All of these are really a means of escape, running away from the problem. Then he usually comes back with phony apologies and tries to work things out.

What happens as a consequence of a "bad fight," when avoidance becomes the rule of life, when conflict is glossed over? Primarily, what happens is that all of the hostility and all of the anger just stays inside. In some cases it literally burns out stomachs with ulcers and in other cases we have heart problems or many other physical and emotional problems which are associated with too much hostility, too much anger held inside. The hurts and strains may be reflected in in-law tensions, money handling, child rearing, and sex adjustments, to name just a few possibilities. How tragic it becomes when couples pretend that everything is all right when it is not; when they try to convince themselves that the conflict is only a passing thing, when it keeps gnawing away at their feelings of well-being. The anger and hostility just does not disappear by itself — it remains, it smolders, it deepens, and in many cases it ultimately explodes. Often when it explodes, it explodes too hard and conciliation and reconciliation are no longer possible. The couple ends up in the divorce court, or the marriage may remain structurally intact but functionally broken. Divorces are never caused by "good fights," fights that settle things, but divorces are always caused by communications that are not finished, that aren't complete.

A "good fight" or "constructive conflict" differs from a "bad fight" in many ways. Most significantly, a "good fight" is an argument that continues until it settles something. In other words, no one runs away to escape from it. The issues at stake are talked through completely. When this occurs, something pretty marvelous begins to happen because basically most of us are sensible people. When persons are angry, when they are shouting at each other, or even talking quietly in disagreement, the adrenalin really begins to pump and at this point one begins to exaggerate tremendously. However, this can continue only so long. Moreover, since we can stay angry for only so long, as one begins to listen to himself and to each other, a sense of humor takes hold and the husband may say to his wife, "Honey, maybe I went a little too far with those last statements." Then with everything out on the table, on the surface, out in the open, apologies can be made and real communication can begin. These are the characteristics of a "good fight." It results in good communications because the characteristics have to do with listening, with being honest, with talking about everything that is important, with love, and finally admitting honestly that not all of the problems we face can be solved on a rational basis. We are emotional people, deeply emotional, and sometimes we have a real need to release these emotions, even if it is in a "good fight."

The discussion centering on "good" and "bad" fights leads us to some important, concluding generalizations. The method we use to raise issues in the family is very significant. Certainly it would be impossible to approach every issue with a smile on our face; this could be basic dishonesty. However, in communication, how one says something, and the verbal content of the message are often much more important than the intent of the communicator or sender. To successfully raise and solve issues in conflict, care should be exercised so that the conflict can be conciliated without disrupting or destroying the deeper relationship. This will require communication in a spirit and attitude which gives promise of a better future relationship. One needs to learn the art of communicating his own real feelings to another. As we discussed previously, all persons have a conflict with authority, therefore, condemning, blaming, castigating, charging, attacking, and coercing will definitely prohibit an understanding relationship from developing. Moreover, some approaches to conflict resolution are almost guaranteed to end in failure. Accusations without a chance to respond, a vindictive tone of voice, nagging, constant complaining, moralizations, self-protectiveness, and authoritarianism almost always ensure failure in the problem-solving method.

We need to be reminded today that love is a tremendous thing; it is almost unbelievable how strong the love for man and woman can become once they have lived through a few years of marriage. It becomes almost an irresistible and unbreakable thing and we should trust it more.

It appears that one of the reasons why persons do not communicate with each other more is that they are afraid. One is afraid that if he talks frankly and openly about things to his partner, she would leave. This is a ridiculous fear. The reason marriages break down is *not* that spouses talk so frankly, but simply that they do not talk at all. It would be reasonably safe to say that 100 percent of persons seeking professional help have basic problems in communication. So we need to keep talking and trust love more.

For Summary and Review

1. What do persons hope to achieve by avoiding communication in marriage?
2. What are the characteristics of "good" communication?
3. What are the characteristics of "bad" communication?
4. What are the negative consequences of playing the game of "let's pretend"?
5. What is meant by the statement that for communication to be complete, "both must talk with love"?
6. Do you agree with the author's concept of "the good fight"? Why? Why not?
7. Discuss: "Divorces are never caused by a 'good fight'."
8. What approaches to problem solving are almost guaranteed to result in failure?
9. Why do couples need to "trust love more"? Explain!
10. List the strengths and weaknesses of this chapter. How could the discussion of the concepts be improved?

Chapter 4

Improving Communication

How may communication in marriage be improved? There is no formula, no short cut, no easy automatic way. Marriage partners need to learn the skills of communication because the most important things in marriage are learning how to talk to one another and secondly, how to talk to oneself – to look introspectively at oneself.

As couples begin seriously and deliberately to improve their communication, their relationship may become more difficult for awhile instead of experiencing immediate improvement. There is a simple reason for this fact. The reason is basically that the individuals involved are real people and they are living in a real marriage; and there just are not any easy answers when real people and real communication are involved. It is difficult for one to look at himself and ask, "How do I constantly try to improve me?" It is likewise a complex job for each to look at his or her partner and ask, "How do I build her or how do I build this man?" The questions are, however, very important and one must be consciously aware of them at all times during marriage. This chapter will point out some of the pitfalls couples can be consciously aware of as they deliberately seek to improve their marriage relationship through better communication.

Probably the best place to begin is with you/me. The ever present danger to communication is our own ethnocentrism

(I am always right), our own self-conceit, and our own egocentrism (self-centeredness). What we sincerely believe is that the problem and the solution is for our mate to change; we are good communicators. Many couples who come to the professional marriage counselor are in deadly earnest as they ask for help to "straighten out the 'old lady' or the 'old man'." Without a doubt, the best marriage manual ever written, the New Testament, deals with this problem very directly and bluntly, yet so discernedly. Christ talked about a mote and a beam, or one might say a speck of dust and an entire tree. If you are not familiar with this illustration, listen carefully! He said in effect, don't look for the speck in the other person's eye, look for the log in your own eye. This is a simple but basic point in improving communications in the home (Matthew 7:3; Luke 6:41).

One of the things most people have to look at in themselves is *sarcasm.* Most of us are sarcastic persons. It seems to be easy, if not in fact enjoyable, for us to be ready to give to someone else a glib, sarcastic dig in the ribs, where it hurts. However, sarcasm is a tremendously damaging thing in the marriage relationship. A sarcastic person is usually a hostile person, sometimes quite aggressive; and if the person is not fully aware of himself, he may punish the ones he really loves and cares about the most. The sarcastic person may over a period of time develop as Roy Fairchild labels it in his book, *Christians in Families,* "a sensitivity to the evil in others." The sarcastic person may also develop unconsciously a pharisaical attitude toward himself which includes the feeling: "God, I thank You that I am not like other men." If this happens, one with ease discovers all of the shortcomings of other people and consciously and unconsciously seeks to remind them of their shortcomings and their inadequacies.

If communication has become a one-sided process, with no response from one's spouse, and the person is complaining about the other, a careful evaluation needs to be made to discover whether or not the reason is sarcasm. Good communication requires both an individual with something important to say, and one who is expected to and willing to listen; both must be motivated to try to improve their mutual communication. If one is sarcastic, this becomes an impossibility.

Sometimes, what we label as "a good sense of humor" is in reality an excuse we use for sarcasm. In our culture, a great deal of "humor" involves making fun of another person. No one would deny, of course, that much of this kind of humor is not destructive. However, in the close, intimate relationship of marriage, when things aren't going so well anyway, and when good communication patterns have not been developed, this kind of humor can cut a spouse apart and make him feel cheap and inferior. Because sarcasm hurts too much, communication between the couple becomes impossible when it is used.

How does one face up to the fact that he is too sarcastic? We have a real problem because no one likes to think of himself as being sarcastic. There really is only one test; it is basically a simple one. The test is this: One must keep on asking himself how would I feel, or how would I like to have this said to me in exactly the same way? In other words, we need to listen to ourselves as if we were the other person. This is how we discover sarcasm in ourselves. It may not be easy, but we need to do it constantly and deliberately.

Nagging is another barrier to good communication. All of us are prone to nag at times. Like sarcasm it can be a good thing at times or a very bad thing. We can be both sarcastic and nagging without being aware of it. If we are aware, the temptation is to kid ourselves about our reasons for doing it. Nagging possibly is a symptom of the basic problems in communication between the couple on the one hand, and/or a habit pattern one has learned from childhood training and experience on the other hand. Moreover, when we add to this the basic conflict with authority all persons have, as we discussed in the previous chapter, the potential for a great deal of conflict is present.

To help us understand adequately the many facets of nagging, we must define it. A dictionary definition includes the following concepts: Nagging involves bothering, annoying, repeatedly urging, scolding, carping (finding fault unreasonably, complaining), harassing, to keep in a state of agitation or discomfort continually, to impinge on one's consciousness continually an idea, ache, image, etc. The key words probably are *continually* and *consciousness.* Therefore, to nag at a person without let-up, to fight until one gives in, is a behavior that does not face up to the issues squarely or completely. When nagging does become high on the list of the spouse's complaints, the most probable reason is her/his failure to give a complete hearing about the things that matter to the other and it remains an unsettled issue constantly in the forefront of the person's concern and consciousness.

Nagging takes many forms. People may be nagged with sweetness; people are nagged by nagging itself; people can be nagged by illness, by feigned tiredness; people can be nagged by a quiet presence of the other person, to name just a few important examples. What all nagging has in common is the fact that it annoys, irritates, and disturbs the other person.

Even though most dictionaries identify nagging as a female trait, some experts feel that men are the worst offenders. Most men would not like to admit to the fact because our culture also implies that this is an unmasculine behavior. However, how many times doesn't the man, especially early in marriage, help his wife to become a better person by reminding her to do the dishes right after dinner, explaining to her how his mother used to cook and keep the house? In other words, he is telling her what he would like her to become. Nagging may not be a nice word for it, but this helping each other in the above way is nagging, according to the dictionary definition above. As one looks carefully at the definition and the examples given, a significant fact comes to light. Nagging is immature behavior engaged in by persons because they have not learned the skills of interpreting their own feelings to the other, or to each other. Nagging is used because one has not learned to empathize (totally understand) with one's mate.

We can test our empathy and learn a good deal about ourselves and others. Since introspection must precede an understanding of the other person, one needs to be aware of the following evaluative points in his or her mental and behavioral processes. So that these points will be most meaningful and useful they will be placed in question form. Do I observe tact (skill in avoiding what would offend or disturb) in my relationship with my spouse? Do I drive through my own ideas, plans, and wishes? Do I overrule all responses and objections of my spouse? Do I experience satisfaction from my dominance (control of all decisions)? Do I experience satisfaction and happiness when I get my own way? Do I usually express forceful opinions to my spouse? Am I guilty of assuming that my spouse agrees with me, my ways and my decisions? Am I a good listener so that I hear what my spouse is really saying? Do I usually display an apathetic response to my spouse's needs, wishes, and conversation? Do I read personal references into everything that is said? If the answer is yes, this recognition should help one at least to make a beginning toward refraining from the nagging and bickering which destroys good communication. If the behavior indicated in the questions is severe enough, and if it goes on for an extended period of time, it will condition our partner not to respond, nor to listen, and communication will be totally destroyed.

Dishonesty in communication is another practice which most persons engage in over and over again as they talk to each other. Exploitative dishonesty can be frustrating and damaging because persons may become aware of its purpose and realize its untruth. Men sometimes are pretty dishonest about flattery, especially flattery for sexual reasons. Too often it includes a selfish motivation. The man comes home at night and sees his wife in the kitchen. Her hair is all stringy, she is dressed in a pair of stained shorts she once used to paint the garage, and an old sweatshirt that was brand new several years ago. She really looks a mess. So what does he say? "Wow, you look sweet, honey." He, of course, is thinking about later on tonight. This is really a basically dishonest approach.

Women also use this approach when they want the man to do something. Exploitative dishonesty in many instances is a heritage from the dating period and is a sign of immaturity and insecurity. As such, it involves pretending, keeping one's mate guessing, the need for reassurance, and the need for constant testing of his love. If flattery is used only when the one desires something from the other, the obvious consequence is doubt. Marriage and good communication need calm emotional security. In a happy marriage, both partners need to express and demonstrate their love so that neither one has the occasion for doubt. Flattery as an expression of love for one's mate which implies that: "I love you as a person, I care and am concerned about you, because you are you, regardless of your dress, hairdo, or housekeeping skills." This is constructive. Flattery which implies a favor really says: "I will love you if you provide what I want," and is therefore destructive for the person. The idiom: "Flattery will get you nowhere" is really quite perceptive. It is necessary to have honest flattery, but if it is not honest it really will not work.

Most persons need to stop running away from communication. *Avoidance* of communication only serves to hurt the marital relationship. Avoidance is a common reaction because it is natural for persons who sense a difference between themselves to move apart: to keep out of contact, to grow silent, to change the subject, or not to hear what has been communicated. Many times it is not only the emotional escape that we seek, but also we run away physically so that we do not have to confront each other and resolve the difference or misunderstanding. One might say that humans are ingenious in devising ways of staying away from communication which might result in the resolution of a problem.

Many specific examples can be given for purposes of clarification. One of the more commonly used methods is to get involved in "good activities." We get so busy, very busy, so that we cannot sit down to talk things out. The wife wants to sit down to have a talk and the husband replies: "Sorry, honey, I can't tonight, I'm too busy; I have an important meeting." In our society, it appears that sometimes anyway, most of the meetings we feel we have to go to, most of the important issues in society we need to solve, have been created specifically for the purpose of keeping us so busy we don't have time to confront the ones closest to us. It might be possible that if we first confronted each other at home in real honest communication many of the needs of our society could be met and we could eliminate some of the important meetings. There is no doubt that the P.T.A., Boy and Girl Scouts, Young Adult groups, etc., serve useful and functional purposes in our society. But if they simply become to a specific individual a way of running away from the problems in the home that need resolution, for this person and his marriage, they become destructive.

Marriage counselors observe that many marriages which on the surface appeared to be nearly perfect, suddenly come apart at the seams. Everyone in town "knew" the marriage was good. Why did the marriage fall apart? The most plausible explanation gleaned from counseling records is that even though the couple lived together for many years, the two people hardly knew each other. Dad is out on Monday, Tuesday, and Wednesday nights doing all kinds of good things for other people's kids and families or community. Mom is out on Thursday, Friday evenings and Saturday afternoon doing wonderful things such as church work, cooking for the local bazaar or soup supper, Girl Scouts, Cub Scouts, and all kinds of good things. In the process of helping others the two are totally avoiding the needed communication between themselves. Isn't it interesting how much we talk to other people and how little we talk to each other in marriage? This is a basic dishonesty to each other and a behavior to which most people are prone because we all like to feel that we are saving the world.

There are other specific ways persons use to avoid communication with each other. Television is a significant means of escape today in many homes and especially for many males. The husband comes home at night, flicks on the T.V. and the next time he talks to anyone, he sort of growls at his wife that it is time to go to bed, or something of the kind. Feigning tiredness is one means of escape which is becoming increasingly important in our busy world. Some people get tired any and every time they are confronted with differences and the need to work them out. The tragedy of this habit of avoidance is that the only time when real communication in the home could be developed (when the couple is together) is blocked out and replaced instead by silent, sulking hostility.

Another common method of avoidance is what we will call "the conspiracy of silence." It is really a conspiracy because it involves a mutual non-verbal agreement which in context says: "When we feel a difference or disagreement, we won't express it. We will gloss it over. We will move away from it; it's safer that way." In essence it implies: "You go your way and I will go mine," and then she often devotes full time to her house or her children while he devotes full time to his job or avocation. The consequence of this behavior is that each time there is a difference it remains unresolved. Both live in a completely separate sphere of life. Communication does not and cannot exist and the biblical concept of partners becoming "one-flesh" in marriage is denied.

Once a person has thoroughly looked at himself, it becomes necessary to look at the other person, the one to whom he is married. A hard close look is required so that we will be able to understand this "uncommunicative" partner of ours; the person who won't sit down and talk about things that are so important. We need to ask ourselves, *why?*

For purposes of analysis, we will identify two polar types of individuals: "The strong, silent type" and "the compulsive talker." At some point along the continuum (between the two extremes) each person will find himself. First, "the strong, silent type" is one who pouts instead of talking, who really doesn't do much talking at all; and to try to get him to talk is like pulling teeth without an anesthetic. If your spouse is like this, it is important for you to know why. Why is he this way? By looking at his background one will find out that he has learned to be "a strong, silent type." Some place along the line he was taught and he learned that it does not pay to communicate, especially to women. Perhaps he had a sarcastic mother or father at home and every time he opened his mouth to talk this sarcasm would strike him right in the face. Possibly there was a mother who was too busy to talk to him when he was a child; or for some reason or the other, he now tends to be a very quiet, unresponsive person.

The most important subsequent question is: Now what do you do about it? Unfortunately, often because of frustration and a deep desire to talk to her husband, the wife may use the wrong approach which reinforces his previous learning and causes even further withdrawal. The first time he tries to express himself and his thoughts in his quiet way, the temptation is to say: "Speak up, for heaven's sake! Don't keep constantly moping around, quit your blubbering, say what you mean, get it out in the open!" In most cases, this is the last thing the quiet person needs to hear. Rather, he needs support and encouragement because he has a hard struggle with words; he has a hard time getting it out. If one will just let the "strong, silent types" talk and if we will show them that we are interested, that we are listening, that we are sympathetic and then if we give them enough time to talk their ideas through, then they will have a good experience with talking and gradually they will want to communicate more. It will require patience, a good deal of love, a good portion of acceptance, and much understanding.

What do you do if you are married to a "compulsive talker"? Some persons yak-yak-yak constantly. Perhaps the most irritating thing about a "compulsive talker" is that he keeps repeating himself over and over again. There is an understandable reason for this. Almost all "compulsive talkers" feel that people don't understand them; therefore, to get it straight, to communicate if you will, they feel the need to explain themselves over and over again. What do you say to the "compulsive talker" — the one who is talking all the time and is saying little? "All you ever do is yak, can't you be quiet for awhile?" This cannot help because just as the "strong, silent types" learned to be as they are, the "compulsive talkers" learned to be as they are. Instead, if one lets them talk, lets them know they are being understood and that one is interested in what they are saying, soon the need to talk all of the time is diminished. Obviously, both illustrations are over-simplifications of a more complex situation; however, they serve to demonstrate important problems in communication because, actually, there is no more potentially satisfying combination than the two in marriage when one partner is rather silent and the other rather compulsive. The two could help each other to become balanced communicators. However, the only way they can do this is by encouraging each other to talk and then to listen.

To conclude our discussion on communication it would be helpful to make a few generalizations which will direct the reader toward improving communication. Poor communication is more prevalent than good communication. There generally is a good deal of superficial conversation, but little or no down-to-earth talking going on in marriage. The first thing which needs to be done is to take a look at why. Most communication problems in the home are based on fear, a fear that love is not strong enough to weather the differences and that the marriage might fly apart if the differences are brought out into the open and discussed. Neither is true. Love and marriage never break down because people honestly communicate. Rather, love and marriage break down because people do not communicate. So trust love, it's stronger than you think.

Secondly, to start working on communication in an adult

way requires honesty. Begin by acknowledging your own failure and responsibility and that you know you went too far; and that you are tired of scrapping. Then listen. Allow your partner to unload what is on his mind. Then communication can begin in an adult, mature way. Listen to the little things first, or the big things won't come out.

And finally, if something is wrong with your communication, with your spouse, there is only one place to look — and this is to look at "me" because "me" is the basis for every marriage.

For Summary and Review

1. In improving communications in the home, the best place to begin is with "me." Why?
2. Why is the New Testament the best marriage manual ever written? Explain and illustrate.
3. What major problems do the following present to good marriage adjustment?
    a. Sarcasm
    b. Dishonesty
    c. Nagging
    d. Avoidance
4. How can one discover and work through the above (Item 3) in one's life?
5. What major concepts are identified in the discussion about "the strong, silent type" and "the compulsive talker"?
6. List and discuss the concepts in this chapter that could be expanded and improved.

Chapter 5

A Complicated Me

In this chapter we will discuss some of the factors significant for helping us to understand ourselves and that directly determine the level of adjustment made in marriage. As it is beyond the scope of this chapter to discuss all of the factors, we will be selective. The factors we will use are considered by the author to be fruitful for self-examination on a conscious level by either putting them into effect in one's life or avoiding them. The reader is asked to approach the issues as one who is motivated and concerned about adequate preparation for his own marriage. The discussion will be unavoidably generalized so that flexibility, innovation, creativity, and imagination are not only possible, but desirable, because no marriage is a combination of the same personality configurations. Every marriage is unique because unique persons are involved, even though culture does exert some pressure toward similarity. With this introduction, we will consider some of the factors within marriage and the family that need to be understood to enhance the person's contribution to the marriage experience.

Two unique personalities are involved in a marriage. Most of their characteristics are common to all human beings; however, they also have individual differences due to their sex, inheritance, ideas, feelings, and attitudes acquired as a consequence of their experiences in a particular family and social group. The kind of marriage they have and its quality will, to a considerable degree, depend upon the kind of people they are.

It is important that each spouse understands his/her motivations for behavior. Self-understanding and self-acceptance are, therefore, a basic requirement for all good interpersonal relationships. Adaptability is necessary in all relationships and especially after marriage when differences often become more important and it is no longer possible for each spouse to go separate ways to avoid them.

Some of the adaptations and adjustments that are nearly universal and not unique are: methods of handling finances, use of leisure time and recreation, religious expression and behavior, demonstration of affection, choice of friends, intimate relations, getting along with in-laws, separation and togetherness, manners and etiquette, life values and goals, and the training and discipline of children. The relevant question to ask is this: "What is our approach and response to the above adjustment areas found in marriage?"

The objective of this chapter is primarily to help the reader bring to the conscious level those things that condition and direct behavioral responses. This results in a better understanding of the truth that what goes into marriage determines what comes out of it. The most important things going into marriage are attitudes, preferences, aversions, habit patterns, and emotional response patterns which give to or deny to the couple the aptitude of compatibility and adaptability. Happy marriages are built and are always in the process of becoming because marriage is a dynamic, continuing relationship. Unconscious motivation is the major concern of this discussion as we attempt to help the reader create self-understanding and self-awareness. Too often one is not aware of his true motivation and is likely to make up reasons for his actions.

Conditioning accounts for most of our fears, tastes, and attitudes. Most of the responses we make are built up. All behavior has its antecedents in or is the result of many contributing factors or roots. The individual is the product of his experiences and whether these be large or small none is ever lost. When an individual is confronted with a new situation, he reacts according to his previous conditioning and experiences.

With the foregoing abbreviated and oversimplified descriptions well in mind, we are challenged to recognize a very significant fact which affects married couples directly. Two people are married. They come to each other with the same drives or needs, but with different motivations, energies, expectations, conditioning, and experiences. Every adjustment in marriage, therefore, requires an understanding of self, an understanding of the other, and a mutual understanding and agreement for the present. It becomes obvious at this point that conflict in marriage will be normal. William G. Sumner termed the association of the sexes in marriage as being "antagonistic cooperation." Conflict in marriage can be removed or reduced by the other person changing, by changing oneself, or by some form of compromise. It is not the conflict or the disagreement in marriage that poses the major problem; rather the manner in which it is expressed and worked out that causes the greatest difficulty and this is where self-understanding becomes a crucial need.

The remainder of this chapter will be devoted to helping the reader to begin looking at himself so that he may develop the insight needed to be a better married person. The concepts and illustrations reinforce the introductory materials and are reality-oriented in that they direct one's thinking to common (although not always recognized as such) interrelational problems made complex because of our past conditioning and experiences.

One of the most sacred institutions we have ever invented in our society we will call "Dear old mom/mother." Specifically, it is an institution which also includes other close relationships such as father, brother, sister, uncles, aunts, and other people we grew up with and who were a part of our background and our early experiences. This "myth of motherhood" does more damage to the human personality than perhaps any other thing could possibly do. We have a special day called "Mother's Day" and we go to church and hear this good sermon about mothers. Everyone loves, or is supposed to love, "dear old mom." She is always supposed to be patient, gentle, loving, kind, long-suffering, pleasant and agreeable. At least, this is the way she is painted in American mythology and one can recall many other beautiful songs and poems about mother.

With this kind of almost deification of mom, can we really feel that this gal was and is a human being? I think not. The consequence is often that we feel a tremendous amount of guilt because of the big myth of the "perfect" mother or father. This becomes especially true when from our own experience we discovered that she or he was a real "beast" in many ways. We need to face this myth realistically if we can.

First, it would be fruitful for each of us to stop for a moment and answer thoughtfully the following questions. If you are already mothers or fathers, the questions become even more meaningful. Are you always patient? Are you always gentle? Are you always kind? Are you always long-suffering? Are you always agreeable? The answers to the questions in almost all cases will be no. In other words, you will really be saying, "I am human" and the reference becomes significant. Weren't your father and mother also human and what is wrong about our facing our real feelings about them? Moreover, how about facing them with a little humor, a little color, and a little understanding? Surely mom was a bit of a crab at times, dad did nag too much, but maybe there was some reason for it, maybe good reasons which we really never looked for or understood, maybe they never found themselves completely either. Maybe they did the very best they could with what they had to work with. And, maybe it's "me" who is responsible for "me" and we then need to laugh at ourselves when we are acting in a crazy way because we have been conditioned or trained to act that way.

In other words, why can't we take charge of this marriage? Unfortunately, the examples which come out of marriage counseling and family life work do not seem to indicate this success for most people in the past. Most people continue to act entirely as they were conditioned to behave without understanding why they act as they do. What we need to recognize is that we have lived in homes for a long period of time and in these homes we learned how to think, how to act, and more importantly how to feel. Specifically, we formed and learned habits that carry over into our adult experience. If our home was a comfortable place to be generally, then probably we grew up to be quite "comfortable" persons. If our home was an uncomfortable place to be, then certainly we grew up to be persons who are not too pleasant to be around. We need to take a clear look at mom and dad as they really existed and now exist if we want to learn about and understand ourselves. Most of us have had severe emotional conflicts with mom or dad at some point in our relationships which resulted in hostile feelings. Here is where a great deal of our problem rests because we are not able to view our parents as real people who have real feelings, and about whom we have real feelings.

Mother is a person, father is a person, our brothers and sisters are persons, and so too are all these people we have lived with in our homes. They have given us our habit patterns, and I think we have to start looking at them realistically. These are people who have taught us, in essence, how to feel about them. Mother by her actions taught us how to feel about her. How can this be? It can be simply because of the fact that you and I are composed of body, mind, and soul. We are composed of two distinct parts – our reason and our emotions. Reason is a part of our mind. Emotion is a product essentially and basically of the body. The emotions we have are features that have been built into us by the persons who were closest to us in childhood.

Let's go back to mom, remembering we are talking about the whole family. Mom lived with dad and she had experiences with dad; she had some kind of love relationship with dad and if she was a person who was much loved by dad, then she was a comfortable person to be around. In a sense, the human being can be compared to a puppy that was given to a little boy. He was a mean little boy. Suppose that this little boy slaps and kicks at the puppy and generally pushes it around in a rough way. Further, suppose this puppy grows up in this environment and then is given to another little boy who loves and adores the dog and is very kind to this puppy. Now, what happens? The puppy will respond to the kindness, but whenever the kind boy makes a fast move in the puppy's direction, the puppy ducks, backs away and is frightened. Most of our emotions are conditioned in the same way in our homes. When mother is around, we duck. When father is around, we duck; we are fearful, frightened, and angry. Why? Sometimes we don't know why. The simple fact is that this is the way we have been conditioned by them in our childhood.

Examples of conditioning are seen in every case of counseling. For example, I imagine everyone knows of a woman who is "crazy clean." The type of gal who is constantly running around the house picking up, dusting the furniture, searching the corners for dirt, etc. Why, one might ask? The answer is that the practice comes out of her childhood conditioning. This woman is never satisfied with herself, nothing is clean enough, nothing is ever good enough for her. Why is this true? Again simply because nothing was ever clean enough for her mom. When one goes back into her childhood, what is found?

The following description is heard so often in the counseling office that it has almost become routine. The little girl cleaned up the house to what she thought was shining bright; and then mother came home. Mother was having a few problems with dad. There was no real love relationship in the home so mother was severely critical and sarcastic. As she walked into the house, the little girl ran up to her and said: "Mommy, I cleaned the house for you." And mommy said: "Yes, that is fine, dear. *But* you left some dust in the corners. Can't you ever clean things right?" This kind of experience repeated many times results in a conditioning to have an obsession with cleanliness. Or the child may react negatively and be conditioned not to want to care if things are clean. However, another kind of conditioning also takes place. She is conditioned to know that any time she is in the presence of her mother she can expect to be struck by the blow of words, to be criticized or belittled as a person. This conditioning will bring a specific response from many alternatives. It could bring avoidance, hostility, or worse, an overt unconscious feeling resulting in emotional problems which may continue throughout the child's life.

Let's take a moment to relate the foregoing illustration to marriage because it has everything basically to do with marriage. The things our emotions have been taught through conditioning in the home has everything to do with how husbands and wives get along together in the home. For example, in many marriages, the man does not believe that women can think, that they know anything. They are impossible to talk to. He believes they are nice to have around, but are definitely inferior. He has learned this from a relationship with his own mother that could never congeal. It comes from a mother who never talked to the boy or who was always too busy. He came to the conclusion that women are superficial, they are lightweights; and it was no use to talk to them; and he really is not conscious of where the idea came from. It came directly out of his emotions which have been trained and conditioned.

Another example of how conditioning works can be found in the woman who is constantly suspicious of her husband. If she had her way, he would never be permitted out of her sight for a moment. She calls the office every day to see if he is there. She always accompanies him when he goes away for meetings, conventions, and for recreation activities. Why does she feel this way? Possibly, dad ran around a bit. This great big, wonderful dad whom she loved as a little girl ran around a bit and she was conditioned to believe that all men run around.

Each and every person has some pre-conceived notion about the opposite sex and his own sex that comes directly out of childhood conditioning. These preconceived, unconscious notions can be tremendously damaging to the marriage relationship. Furthermore, they can also be destructive to our relations with our parents.

The mother-in-law and father-in-law problem is one of the most serious that many couples face in marriage. Why? The most important factor is our guilt over the way we feel toward them. We never quite settle the issues of the problem. Many examples from marriage counseling show that time and time again married people allow mothers and/or fathers practically to take over their marriage simply because they have too much guilt to resist. The reason guilt goes so deep is that we have been so strongly conditioned that we must love mom and pop – and the best way to show this love is not to resist or offend them. Certainly we have to love our parents because God gave them to us as parents, because they are human beings. However, in our culture, love usually has been associated with "good feelings." If one is to be realistic, one discovers immediately that this good feeling is something many persons are not going to be able to have with one or the other of his parents. Marriage counselors have seen many persons destroying themselves by constantly going back to mom and/or pop, trying to find and establish a love relationship based on "good feeling" that they missed out on in childhood. As a result of trying to live in the past, the present is denied, and the future is affected adversely.

A final example of an actual counseling case should help to clarify the concepts of conditioning and guilt. One day a woman came into the office feeling completely evil. For years, whenever she had gone to visit her mother, she felt uncomfortable. She constantly expected to be criticized and experienced a deepening desire to mend this relationship because she felt so guilty about it. She felt that everyone else loved their mother, but she did not. One day she decided to bake her mother a birthday cake. She correctly and beautifully frosted and decorated it with a big "I love you" across the top. Rather hastily she wrapped it in a package and quickly went to visit her mother. She was very excited and hoped that today would be the day they could finally get this difference settled. She walked into the house and brought the cake into the kitchen and placed it on the table. Her mother looked at it and her face turned noticeably sour. The woman said: "Mother, I brought you a birthday cake" in happy expectation and anticipation. Mother replied: "It is very beautiful, *but can't you ever learn to wrap things right?"* One could almost predict the impact. The daughter boiled over and called her mother a "so-and-so" without thinking. When she arrived at the office there was this tremendous guilt. "What kind of person am I to say a thing like that to my mother? What kind of person am I to actually feel hatred for my mother?" Was she really any different from you or me when we have conflict with someone close? What kind of persons are we? What is our responsibility here? Where should we stand?

Probably one of the best places to look to find the answer is in the Scriptures. Never, in any verse of Scripture, is there a reference to the fact that one must get that "real good feeling" when he walks into the presence of mom and dad. The emotional thing is a heritage of our Western culture and really has nothing to do with the position we should or need to take toward our parents. What then would a good position be?

We can begin by recognizing that mom and dad are persons like us, who did the best they could with what they had to work with, and for this we owe them honor and respect (Genesis 2:21-25; Luke 2:40-52; Ephesians 6:1-4). We owe them honor and respect because they are our parents, a relationship ordained by God Himself. We owe them honor and respect because they are human creatures of Almighty God. We need to ask at this point a most valid question which focuses our attention on the crucial issue. Which is the better kind of love? The kind of love that we give to a little baby we just love to cuddle. Everyone can love in this way. Or, the kind of love, Christian love, which is difficult to give? This love continues even when our emotional inclination is "fight-fight." The latter is real love because we are doing it consciously and deliberately. We clearly have to learn to love each other. We need to go back to the biblical admonition that we have to "cleave" to each other after we have "left" our parents. This does not mean that we move only physically away from our parents, but we also have to move out of the home emotionally. If our feelings aren't good toward our parents, this we cannot help. We can, however, help what we do about these feelings.

Thus far we have defined and demonstrated through illustration the fact that self-understanding begins with a recognition that we are what we are because of a long period of learning and conditioning. All of us have had many experiences, both related and unrelated, which have conditioned us and trained the non-thinking part of us, the part that acts almost automatically. In other words, the habits of behavior and response and thinking trained by the home, the school, the church, and the community are a real part of each of us. It would be good if each of us could look back and see the many facets of our conditioning and be able to say honestly and seriously that this is going to be a problem we have to try to overcome. I must face up to the facts of what was good and what was bad and do what I can to build on the good and correct the bad. This is a difficult thing to do because of all the myths surrounding the home in mid-twentieth-century America. But it is important and even imperative that we stop worrying about what a bad person we are. We must put more emphasis on some of the qualities that we think and know are bad for us in our marriage and make them positive and good by putting them to constructive work.

Henry Bowman, in his text *Marriage for Moderns* (Sixth Edition, Reading 11), gives a few suggestions that can be helpful in developing an understanding of ourselves. These suggestions are constructive to use in evaluating many of the conditioned factors which affect our responses to others. The reading is entitled, "When does an adult need to change" and presents some of the signals we should watch for in our own lives. All signals are types of previous conditioning or habits over a long period of time. Obviously, if a person identifies any of the signals as his or her special problem, rapid and immediate change cannot be expected. Rather they should be viewed as a continuous developmental task with a future orientation as reconditioning takes place. I will only summarize briefly the most significant points.

If a person *resists change* and resists it strongly, if he resents suggestions, is defensive in holding to his present ways, clings to the status quo even when outdated, and becomes very rigid, he needs to ask himself, why? Does he fear flexibility, humility and self-searching? Cannot a balance between self-determination and the good of all be struck?

A person may need to change if he discovers that he gets the most emotional satisfaction out of minor virtues, such as orderliness, cleanliness, and *systemizes everything* and all people. If he discovers that the extreme in fact does exist he needs to ask himself, why? Does he fear making mistakes? Does he fear granting freedom and initiative to others? Does he make a fetish of perfectionism, a goal of domination and a wish to oversupervise those around him? The other extreme or polar type would be the one who is *underorganized.* The unorganizer is one who is in a usual state of confusion. The same question needs to be asked. Why? Does he resent discipline? Does he have clearly defined goals? Are his work habits or behavior patterns unconsciously defective?

Many persons *resent evaluation* of themselves by others and cling to the present. They are often engulfed in busy work, rather than looking forward through planning for the future. Or the other extreme of only *dreaming* and more dreaming, and never touching reality can also be very limiting and destructive because one soon loses a sense of proportion and of reality. So again the question must be asked. Why?

One might also find that he needs to change if he is caught in the habit of *condemning things and people.* A great deal of time and emotional energy can be consumed in this habit. Realizing that all is not perfect, one must be alert to the fact that excessive criticism does bring a negative outlook on life. Negativism, suspicion, and fear may become very destructive habits if the progression cannot be halted. It has been suggested by several authors that the "habit of happiness" is one of the most important factors related to happy marriages. Likewise, a negative outlook on life can be one of the factors related to unhappy marriages. Consequently, if one finds in himself the habit of condemning things and people, he should ask himself, Why?

A person may need to change if he is a *perpetual worrier.* A vicious cycle can become evident when worrying is carried to the extreme. One who develops the habit feels lonesome without it and then worries about his habit of worrying. Worrying, of course, cannot be talked out of existence, but a consciousness of the habit pattern can reduce worry after the original problem has been solved, removed or outlived. Again the question which needs to be asked is, Why? Why does one worry so much?

Sarcasm is another symptom – for the sting of it indicates some need for change on the part of the individual. Often, after one has developed the habit and practiced it for years, he may not be aware of the destructive impact which sarcasm has. There are basically two kinds of sarcastic "digs." One is made in the presence of the other and said with a smile; the other "dig" is made behind the other person's back. The very real problem is that unless one is consciously aware of his sarcasm he may mistake it for humor. One must be aware that our culture conditions one very subtly in the use of sarcasm and it is sometimes used as a method of self-defense and/or preservation of self-righteousness. Why then are we sarcastic?

Procrastination is another signal that change is in order. Too often this can become a sign of indecision, an unwillingness to assume responsibility and an unconscious desire to be dominated by someone else. One needs to be more than a reflection of another's wishes, needs, fears, and hopes. The polar characteristic of procrastination, making a fetish out of *quick* decisions, may be even more difficult to live with and change. This type of habit often results in many mistakes, insensitivity to others, and authoritarianism. A definite conflict with authority is likely to develop. How can one develop empathy when compulsion is practiced? What will be the consequences? What will happen when one is unconcerned about agreement among persons whose cooperation may ultimately be needed to accomplish the task considered important?

One of the dilemmas faced by some persons who need to change is found in a subconscious desire to avoid becoming entangled in another person's situation. *Running for shelter* contains many defenses such as being too busy, holding others off by various methods and leaving the problem unheeded. Persons who run away from problems need to ask themselves, Why? No problems in marriage and the family solve themselves; therefore, good adjustment requires facing the problems squarely and then resolving them mutually.

Still another signal for a need to change involves a common behavior of making a *ritual of being frank.* There is honesty which makes possible personal reconciliation and there is a kind of honesty which hurts others. If one finds satisfaction from being frank and watching the hurt response of others, and if he uses frankness to preserve his own self-righteousness at the expense of others, change is necessary. At the extreme, frankness may indeed be an aggressive tendency in the form of psychological sadism.

Change in a person may be necessary if he is *overly suspicious and overly sensitive.* Over-personalization quickly thwarts communication because the person tends to "fly off the handle" as he reads malice into the words and actions of others. He is also quick to respond in self-defense as he views all responses as attacks on himself. The person who *wears his feelings on the proverbial sleeve* needs consciously to attempt to view life more objectively and less personally. He needs to act toward others as though they were friendly. This could lead to some significant change in proving that others can be cooperative.

And finally, the person *who clings to well-earned status* may need to recognize a need to change. Both outside and inside the family, this may be one of the most common of all human relations problems. The sense of being replaced is probably very real. However, one needs to be aware that sometimes a change in status can bring about a great deal more meaning and satisfaction if one prepares to accept it and concentrates more on the new services and the new forms of satisfaction rather than on what has been lost by the change in status. The entire issue surrounding the changes in masculine and feminine roles centers around the fact that many are not prepared to meet the new obligations because the tendency has been for most to cling to the safe, secure, traditional roles.

We have presented only a few of the factors necessary for one to get a better understanding of what makes us click as individuals. We as humans are highly complex and complicated entities. Potentially, each of us can learn to understand himself best if he consciously tries. Unfortunately, marriage is not always the place where we sit down and think logically. It may take each of us a long time before we take a look at ourselves and say: "Look! This is silly. It's time to sit down and talk this thing out and decide where we are going." So we must ask ourselves: "What are we going to do about it? Why do I feel this way? Is it just one of my many conditioned-in factors? Or is it something that has a basis in good honest reason?" We should also ask ourselves, "Is there a better way of doing things than we are now using?

Is this way of mine really reasonable?" By honestly asking these questions and raising these issues it is possible for us better to understand ourselves, handle our feelings and emotions, and get a better understanding of "A Complicated Me."

FOR SUMMARY AND REVIEW

1. The author states that two unique personalities are involved in a marriage. Individual differences do exist but many of the adaptations are nearly universal. What meaning does this have for couples facing adjustment in marriage?
2. Explain: "None of us marries perfection. We only marry human beings."
3. Discuss: "Problems arise in marriage because two different people are taking two different types of conditioning into one relationship." Illustrate and explain.
4. Could marriage be considered as "antagonistic cooperation"? Explain.
5. How did you react to the author's discussion of the "myth of motherhood"? Do you agree with him? Why? Why not?
6. What is the difference between?
   a. Fact
   b. Hang-up
   c. Guilt (give an illustration of each and explain why)
7. The author lists personality characteristics of persons who need to change. Add several you feel should be included in a complete listing. Explain each briefly.
8. Has your concept of "mature married love" changed in any way since you read Chapter 1? If so, in what specific way?
9. How could the church help couples to approach the concepts identified in this chapter, especially guilt?
10. What specific weaknesses did you find in this chapter?

Chapter 6

The Many Meanings of Sexual Intercourse

This chapter is the first of several dealing with sex adjustment in marriage. Sex is a natural human response. Without sex there would be no marriage and it is this element that makes marriage different from all other continuing human relationships. There is much more to marriage than sex; however, it is extremely important in every marriage. Sex is a shared experience and a sharing process with an ultimate goal of mutual need fulfillment and enjoyment, both present and future oriented. Therefore, sex adjustment in marriage is a continuing process which lasts for the lifetime of the persons in marriage. "Time and perseverance" are the essential positive factors in successful sexual adjustment. Impatience and withdrawal are the negative factors leading to poor sex adjustment.

The danger all couples face as they begin their sexual life together is that either they are conditioned to "expect too much" or to not to "expect enough." In this chapter we will look at some of the factors which are important in our conditioning and to do so we will use an analogy of the "perfect love story;" – an almost perfect love story that is, that doesn't happen in enough American homes today.

Sex is a difficult thing to write or talk about to our generation. Our generation is probably more "hung-up" where sex is concerned than any other in modern history. Even though there is a tremendous interest in sexual matters, as the current volume of books and articles crowding the library shelves will substantiate, evidence seems to indicate that we are experiencing more sexual problems than ever before. Homosexuality is increasing; sexual deviance and perversion are more widespread; sadism and masochism are more general in the population; pre-marital pregnancy continues to increase bringing severe emotional, psychological trauma to many young girls and their families; divorce continues to be widespread, affecting as many as one out of four marriages nationally and even more in local areas; an apparent increase in pre-marital sex and delinquency poses a significant social problem. Not all is negative however. Many persons today have adequate knowledge to dramatically improve their sex life and they have been able to reach a much higher level of enjoyment and self-fulfillment. Still, there is a great deal of negative conditioning which takes concerted effort to overcome before the person is capable of experiencing the fullest potential joy of sex in marriage.

It seems that at many points in our every effort to understand human sexuality, we find ourselves at cross purposes with ourselves, at odds with our social institutions of religion, moral codes, law, child-rearing practices, and language. This is further compounded by many "natural" assumptions, the most significant of them being that it is not really possible for males and females to completely understand each other. As a consequence there are many factors which condition and confuse us as we look at the topic of sex.

One of the distortions, a frustration to adequate sexual adjustment which is part of our cultural conditioning, is the labeling of the sexual act as "sin!" Not only before marriage, nor just during the courtship stage, but all through history, sex has been surrounded by sin, shame, and dirtiness. Furthermore, our cultural heritage is that sex is done only in secret, at night, and is primarily enjoyed only by men and that women don't really enjoy it. This so-called Christian idea of sex is ridiculous because certainly it was God's plan for sexual behavior to be a beautiful experience. The concept of "one flesh," for example, implies the idea of a complete and total unity between a man and a woman and sex was given a special meaning and beauty that is found in no other place in human creation. Even though an increasing number of married persons no longer consciously consider sex as evil activity, they do experience repeatedly symptoms of the negative attitudes which come forth in the form of dissatisfaction and disappointment with their sexual relationship (Genesis 1:26-31, 2:18-25, 4:1; Proverbs 5:15-22; Song of Solomon 1:12-2:7, 2:16-17, 4:1-15, 7:1-13; Matthew 19:4-6; Ephesians 5:21-33; 1 Timothy 4:1-5; Revelation 19: 6-8).

Another observation of the sex act found in our culture is that "Sex is a sacred marital duty." Tradition implies strongly that sex is "a masculine right and a feminine duty." Not only is this conditioning reflected in the attitudes of many but also in the many laws of the state statute books. A man in most states may divorce his wife if she refuses to have sexual intercourse; in fact the principle exists that the marriage is not consummated until the sex act takes place. A perversion of the beauty of sex God created occurs when couples approach sex from this duty routine. Sex often becomes a totally disgusting and discouraging experience for both. The "duty routine" is faced so often in the counseling office. It usually goes something like this: "Well, all right, honey, it's Tuesday night again, I suppose you have to have it." And so she sort of mentally sets her alarm clock for five minutes and says: "Please hurry, I've got many things to do that are more important." Sex becomes a thing that has to be done to please the man. This is an old-fashioned, crude, cold attitude toward sex. How much better it would be if we could view sex as a mutual experience, entailing mutual satisfaction, and as an expression of affection, trust and desire by both parties, rather than the imposition of rights and the unwilling performance of duty (See Ephesians 5:22; Colossians 3:9; Titus 2:4; 1 Peter 3:1; Revelation 21:2; Proverbs 12:4; 31:10-31).

The mass media also adversely affects our conditioning toward the sex act. In our modern day, many of the people of our generation have rebelled against the rigid, traditional concepts against sex, and particularly against the idea that sex is sinful, shameful and dirty. However, many have gone to the opposite extreme in their effort to free sex from its negative stereotypes and as a result many, if not most, books we pick up to read are filled with unrestricted sex, with material bordering on pornography, perversion, sadism and really ridiculous and destructive sex. Unfortunately, much of what is produced about sex today in the mass media is written by persons knowing little if anything about sex and the beauties of sex in marriage. The paradox found in the treatment of sex by the mass media is that rather than freeing the person to experience sex as it is potentially possible for a person, it in essence is the same old puritanical, traditional, stereotyped concept. The persons who write these pornographic, perverted, obscene works still view sex as dirty, sinful and shameful.

Even more harmful to many avid readers of sex-filled books and viewers of sex-sodden films at the local cinema is the misleading connotation that sex is only physical and that it can be dealt with entirely on a "pleasure-pain" principle. Unfortunately for the victims of this propaganda, this view is a "romantic illusion." It is so easily accepted by many because on the surface sexual attraction is a physical reaction, but the sexual relationship, even on a very casual level, is not that simple. Sex is a powerful force. Even the current crop of sexually obsessed writers acknowledge this by the fact they dwell on it continuously. However, it involves the whole personality as it involves acceptance, fulfillment, hopes, desire, feelings as well as knowledge of rejection, exploitation and failure. To place sex on a physical level only is to deny to oneself and one's partner the full potential of sex. Intercourse potentially and realistically is symbolic of commitment as a man and woman expose themselves in intimacy to each other; "we belong to each other"; "we are one." Sex involves psychic, spiritual, and emotional elements which lift sex in humans totally above the level of merely animal mating. No one needs to deny that sex on the physical level is fun, pleasurable and needs expressing; however, sex experience can never be perfect unless it involves the mind and the soul as well as the body. Of course man can live at many different levels of fulfillment and completeness. In this book, however, the author's interest is to help the reader maximize his life experience in the area of sexual behavior.

Another troublesome emphasis in the mass media is that sex is natural, so use it. This emphasis on the surface has a ring of correctness and appropriateness. If taken at face value, as the media portrays human sexuality, sex becomes almost entirely individualistic and exploitative. Furthermore, sex becomes a "thing-in-itself" or an "end-in-itself." This facade encourages attitudes toward sex which deny to the other person self-hood; rather, the other becomes segmented and of little worth as a person and is only viewed as a sexual being to be used for pleasure and self-satisfaction. The "playboy philosophy," among other perpetuations of traditional masculine superiority and feminine inferiority, builds on this as a major theme. If there is sin involved in the sexual act, this is where it will be found, as individuals who are much concerned about their self needs, fail to, or refuse to, or are incapable of acknowledging their own self or another as persons based on a biblical precept, "Thou shalt love thy neighbor as thyself." The persons who become aware of the need to respect others in the same way they need to be respected as a person, will be able to build a meaningful, complete sexual relationship with another in marriage other than "just bodies" involved in a physical act.

Finally, we are conditioned by the media, folklore, marriage manuals, and to a degree by our own ignorance and insecurity about sex, to view the sexual act in behavioral terms. A great deal of emphasis is placed on method, procedure, positions, stereotyped foreplay, stimulation, frequency, duration, movements, orgasm, climaxes, etc. The underlying assumption of this attitude is that sex is "what one does" rather than "who one is" as a person. This will be discussed in a later chapter. The importance of methods and skills in love-making are of course significant; however, they can never become really important to the sexual relationship unless they are learned together in the process of mutual need fulfillment accomplished mutually in marital sexual intercourse.

With this brief background in mind, the reader is encouraged to apply the negative conditioned factors to the "perfect love story" that follows. Could the successful relationship have been accomplished if the negative conditioning had been a strong factor in their relationship this day? What characteristics of this day made it successful?

Our love story begins early in the morning with two people who care about each other. They got up from the breakfast table, and maybe they have been kind of quiet. As it is in many homes, breakfast is a tedious affair and perhaps one is not awake enough for much conversation. However, there is a feeling of closeness because they do love each other and care about each other. The interim of silence is a good thing, they are used to it, they need it and want it.

Down at the office (or at work) the day goes perfectly for the man and the woman has a perfect day as well. Everything goes right; her cooking turns out well, the pies don't burn, and the oven did not get dirty. He comes home for lunch at noon and it is a relaxed, joyous period of time. They are glad to see each other. Both have a change from the routines of the day and they sit down and talk about trivial things, about the kids, about the house, about their plans for a picnic outing they hope to enjoy during the weekend.

After lunch is over, they hold each other and caress each other for some time. As they do, they send their little signals for later in the day, looking forward to evening when they will be together again. It has been a good time, a good feeling, a good start for a good day.

And this kind of day continues all through the afternoon. Things continue to go well at the office. The man receives several compliments from his boss for work well done. At home she is thinking about him and as she thinks about him in a loving, caring kind of way, the physical process of sexual intercourse actually begins. The emotional preparation and anticipation began early in the day; now the physical process begins. This is a very important part of the preparation because for a couple to thoroughly enjoy sexual intercourse, the woman needs to be completely ready emotionally and completely lubricated physically. This is not a simple process of pushing this and manipulating that. In most women (as a matter of fact one could say all women), the physical and emotional processes are totally tied together. When the woman feels loved, when she feels needed, when she feels wanted, important and respected as she does this day, the physical lubrication of the vagina actually begins and she senses a certain wetness there. And he too has started his physical processes because he thinks about tonight as being another one of those nights that he and his wife are going to be able to add to their treasury of caring for each other. This thought makes him feel good and comfortable and naturally gives him something of a physical arousal.

Evening arrives; he comes home for dinner. When he arrives at home we find the same kind of a day, a real beautiful day and in some ways unusual. At the dinner table tonight with their three teenage children there was no need to referee a fight, for tonight they were simply charming, the generation gap was not noticeable, they were fantastically interesting and full of fun. They each gave a description of an exciting event in their lives as it occurred today. There was humor, laughing and fellowship. Again there was a feeling of warmth and comfort which are a part of the emotional preparation for both the man and woman for the physical act of sexual intercourse later tonight.

Dinner is completed, the dishes are washed, the evening goes by, and it's relaxing. They sit on the davenport watching T.V. He is holding her, they are enjoying each other, they are caressing each other. Now and then there is a kiss; there are caring, communicating sounds being made to each other, signals they have learned to give and recognize.

For a change, the kids get to bed and are settled down at a reasonable time. This is really unusual in most homes, because in most cases as the man and woman are ready to make love to each other, one of the children wants to sit up and talk. But, this night is different, the kids are in bed and sleeping. And the couple are ready for the love-making.

Before we go on, let's take a look at what has happened. They prepared each other all day long and are looking forward to possessing each other in love-making. They are ready to make love to each other with expectation and anticipation.

So now they go to bed and they begin to possess each other. They hold each other very closely and their sensations become aroused. They get to the point where they want and need each other very much and as they do, their caresses get deeper and stronger. However, they are still kind of slow, lazy, and relaxed and loving because neither is in a hurry tonight. Both sense deeply that this day is for them a perfect day for love-making. There is no hurry, the kids are sleeping, there is no pressure from anything and tonight is the night that they can thoroughly love and enjoy each other.

They are careful not to end this beautiful night too quickly. For example, the man has come to know himself very well and one of the things he has learned about himself is that the most sensitive of his nerve endings, the sexual nerve endings, are located at the tip of his penis. One might call these nerve endings the "sexual trigger" because this is exactly what it is in most men. The nerve endings are there and their purpose is to signal the brain when the wife is ready to receive the semen and sperm. In most respects it is a very simple, uncomplicated process, but one of which men need to be thoroughly aware so that they do not ejaculate prematurely and frustrate their partner.

As sexual intercourse advances normally, the wife does so signal this tip of the penis when she is ready to climax by exerting a drawing, compelling, pressure against the penis. As this message then is translated to the brain, the semen is released and this is how the simultaneous climax is achieved. The penis is not a part of the body with a brain in itself and a man must be conscious of this. It does only what it is told to do. Tonight the man is very careful so he does not press it against her with too much pressure so that he will ejaculate. He has learned from experience that this can be disastrous to the love-making. So he moves slowly and carefully.

He also is very much aware of what is happening to her because this couple has spent many years in developing honest sexual communication. He remembers that at first they had learned the hard way. There had been many hurts, lots of upsets and failures, many frustrations, and at one point she really believed she had married a sex maniac because she was sure that sex was all he ever thought about. However, neither one, of course, had had time to clearly develop an understanding of the other, and they really didn't even know or understand themselves. But somewhere along the line they started talking about their sexual needs and uncertainties. They were able to get it out in the open and each was eventually able to say, "This is how I feel" and "This is what I need and like," and "This is how you can help me to respond." As they did this they came to understand each other, and right now he understands her well.

He knows that she is becoming tremendously excited, but he knows that she is a long way from being ready to receive his penis. He has learned that most women, including his wife, do not respond as fast as men because of their biological and cultural conditioning. Some women respond very rapidly, and if they do, it's wonderful and it is normal. But most women do not arouse quickly simply because of the way they were trained and brought up. He, however, has consciously observed that it takes his wife a certain length of time before she will be able to communicate her readiness to him.

So he knows that, even though she is very excited, she is not ready to receive his penis until she has an irresistible desire to receive it. In other words, when she is ready, this is the time to begin. It took him a while to learn this because, as many young men believe, he believed it his role and masculine responsibility to begin the act of sexual intercourse. Most alert men know what happens when they decide that now is the time. The timing is bad because the penis is hard and firm and the male's reliability is almost completely destroyed. The ejaculation occurs before she is ready to climax and the act is frustrated.

But they have discovered through their communication and observation that this won't work for them. They discover through their experience together that when the penis is inserted too soon while the vagina is still dry and it is not adequately lubricated, that this puts too much pressure on the tip of the penis and the results are disastrous as he ejaculates too soon and frustrates and upsets both his wife and himself. So tonight, before proceeding with the actual act of sexual intercourse, he takes the time to bring her to the point of maximum lubrication and consequently brings her also to the point of having an irresistible desire to receive the penis.

It is important at this point to emphasize the need not to make a "big deal" out of the technique. Very simply stated, the technique you use should be the one you have learned through your experience, communication, and careful observation. Techniques are different for each couple and they are different for each separate sexual experience. A few simple, normal concepts will follow as we continue the story of the "perfect night."

The clitoris of the woman is a small organ that lies at the top of the vagina. Medical people tell us this is in reality a kind of small penis. The clitoris is the most sensitive organ that most women possess as far as their sexual nature is concerned. When the couple approaches the point where they desire each other and then strongly desire each other, the man manipulates or presses or caresses the clitoris and the woman becomes aroused very quickly. Now on this night it's a lazy, relaxed, loving night and maybe he doesn't want to move this fast, maybe he is not so tense himself. So tonight, perhaps, he just plays with her thighs. He has discovered they are very sensitive, she told him they are. Perhaps he kisses and fondles her breasts a while longer. Eventually she reaches the point where she is lubricated and where she does want to receive the penis. Now and only now is the right time for the penis to be inserted.

How does he wait this long? This is a major problem for many American males, maybe most males. There are several ways in which holding back can be and is accomplished. First of all, there is a natural way of holding back and this is by just enjoying and loving each other. For most men, when a woman plays with and caresses the testicles at the base of the penis, a little bit of semen which does not contain any sperm, or a few at the most, is given off. This is a physically relaxing, natural thing as it takes a little bit of pressure off the nerves in the penis. It gives a little bit more time before ejaculation occurs. The second control is a mental-emotional one. A man who cares about and loves his wife and therefore feels this love returned can approach sex more relaxed and with few fears. This confidence in himself which comes when his wife shows confidence in him is a great emotional help and it gives the man the confidence and ability to wait. An additional help is just sort of mentally thinking about something else when the pressure is too great. Tonight the man in our story has no problems with either of the above.

She has played with him, he is physically relaxed and the penis is inserted and intercourse proceeds.

What do they do about position? They get into a comfortable position that they enjoy. There is a notion found in the mass media and folklore that the couple should use many different positions. Our couple have lived through this and they know that for them it is not the position that is really important, but that *sexual intercourse is not what you do, that sexual intercourse is what you are.* And, although they have used the same position for years there is an infinite variety in their sexual intercourse.

So our couple continues the motions of intercourse, in other words, for them it means the penis riding and pressing against the clitoris, the chest against her breast, in a comfortable and enjoyable position, until she approaches her climax. She sends a message to the penis by exerting the pressure we discussed earlier, supplemented by other bodily and verbal communication. The messages go to the brain and he releases the sperm and semen at just a moment later. As he ejaculates, the extra motion causes her to respond with her climax. There would be variation from time to time as some women, most in fact, would be capable of multiple orgasm, whereas the male is not usually capable of rapid multiple ejaculations. Therefore, communication about response and needs is helpful and important. Now this was a good night for our couple, the perfect night, one that doesn't happen too often in most homes.

For a moment, let's take a look at this home as it really is. In our illustration everything worked well. A perfect home, perfect kids, good day at the office, everything 100 percent. How many times do you envision this happening in your home? Why not more often? Basically, of course, it is because we are human beings, our days are complicated because we are very complicated people. We often have hurt feelings, we are often upset, and the children are often something less than angels.

Our second illustration is about the same couple on a different kind of day. It will not be necessary to go through the entire procedure in detail again, but we will look at this day as a tension-filled day. On this particular day a sudden change in the weather has occurred, a snow storm is developing, so you know what the school superintendent does. He does the mother a great big favor, he sends all of her kids home and for the rest of the day they are pulling on her skirt asking mommy how about this and how about that. The teenage boy who was such a clown and so funny at the dinner table the other night, well he is not funny now as he mopes around and keeps saying, "Ma, what is there to do? Ma, what's there to do?" Mom is almost driven to distraction.

The husband has his day at the office. Everything goes wrong. He gets chewed out by the boss. He has a wastebasket full of papers because he hasn't accomplished a thing all day long. So tonight he comes home and he is looking for sympathy and she expects a little too. Instead of both of them being happy, they are hateful and irritable. They glare at each other over the table. The kids get chewed out by dad because he is mad at mom and this goes on for the evening. She prances around the kitchen, slams the pots and pans around in the kitchen as he sits and buries his nose in the newspaper or magazine. Suddenly it's 9:00 o'clock and the thought occurs to him, *Wow! this is really good adult behavior, isn't it?* And so they smile at each other in a weak, sheepish way, they go to bed and then they make love again.

This time, however, their love-making is an apology to each other. They are trying to say to each other, "I am sorry for my immaturity." Does this kind of love-making go 100 percent? Sometimes it does, but this is a real exception because everything that happened to this couple all day long goes to bed with them. All of the troubles the wife had during the day keep the vagina from becoming feminine, from feeling feminine, from having the necessary confidence and anticipation, so it is difficult to lubricate. And the chewing out that the guy got from his boss is still with him as he goes to bed. His confidence is not present and his penis that was firm and hard and ready on this other good, lazy, loving night, is rubbery now. Tonight sexual intercourse is a method, almost a violent physical thing, because they are trying to show each other with the intensity of their love that they really do care. And so tonight it's not much use. They hardly begin when the penis ejaculates. Most couples have experienced this. It is a terrible feeling early in marriage and for some it's a problem many years into marriage.

However, tonight, in this home there is enough love. So she grins up from the pillow, she sort of laughs at him and says, "I guess tomorrow night is the night, John, prepare to defend yourself." And he chuckles too, and he says, "That's what happens when you arouse a sexy woman."

There are many different meanings of sexual intercourse — a lot of meanings for different couples on a lot of different nights. Very seldom does sexual intercourse fit a "textbook" pattern because each person expresses himself in a unique pattern. The best preparation for an adequate, satisfactory sexual adjustment between two people is the conscious development of a healthy, flexible, balanced attitude toward sex, free from all of the unnecessary inhibitions and fears, coupled with sound, reliable information gained from reliable sources. But the important thing that all of us have to keep in mind is that every single thing that happens to us throughout our lives, as well as what happens to us all day long, comes to bed with us at night and makes love with us. In other words, sexual intercourse is not what you do, sexual intercourse is what you are. Consequently, in most respects, every couple's mutual adjustment is unique; therefore, they need to learn to know each other thoroughly, understand each other completely, and respond to each other according to the events in their lives and the mutual needs they experience.

For Summary and Review

1. Creation is a story of love. In what ways is the theme of love and creation related to sexual intercourse?
2. Discuss or analyze the following:
    a. Sex and sin
    b. "One-flesh"
    c. "Marital or wifely duty"
    d. Sex is physical
    e. Sex is natural
    f. Sex is what you do.
3. What important characteristics of human sexual response does the illustration in this chapter identify? Briefly analyze each.
4. Discuss: "Sexual intercourse is not what you do; sexual intercourse is what you are."
5. A French writer once said that sexual intercourse ". . . is the means by which beauty breaks into the world." Elaborate on his statement.
6. Point out the strengths and weaknesses of this chapter.

Chapter 7

Thinking About Sexual Intercourse

INITIAL SEXUAL RELATIONSHIPS IN marriage are extremely significant as they reveal the approach to the lovemaking process which is important in determining attitudes regarding the sex act. Also, at a deeper level, behavior in the sex act is indicative of the attitudes and feelings which the husband and wife express toward one another. Since love-making is "an art," it requires time, patience, thoughtfulness, perseverance, observation, and understanding for its fullest development. Since this is true, there may be discouragement, dissatisfaction, or disappointment. There need not be this feeling if the couple realizes that no humans ever reach perfection in anything; they merely move toward it. They can strive but rarely achieve it. Their biggest problem will be to overcome the temptation to stop trying, to stop working at adjustment, and instead continue to perpetuate their ignorance, attitudes, inhibitions and mistakes. This chapter will deal specifically with some of the barriers to the development of adequate sexual relationships and some thoughts on how to face these barriers more realistically and constructively.

Marriage counselors are often faced with the question: "Why is it that people don't try harder to love one another?" Over and over again one hears the same complaint that there is no romance, no love apparent in the relationship. Men are often heard the complain that they are not "getting enough" at home. Women complain that their husband is just a "cold fish." Why? Why don't people work harder at loving one another? Why doesn't a man give his wife more love? These are such important questions because, when love is given, a healthy, responsible sexual response is received in return. The reasons for withholding love do not make any sense until we look at our training and background for marriage; then the reasons become a great deal clearer. What do most people know about marriage when they get married? Most of us know many things and unfortunately, just about all of them are wrong or at least only half truths at best.

First of all, as we discussed in the early part of the last chapter, many of us learned early in life that sex was a bad and sinful thing associated with two terrible words, fornication and adultery. We were indoctrinated through a "Thou shalt not" approach to sex which essentially treated sex as a gift from God to be used solely for the purpose of procreation. If any pleasure was involved it was purely secondary. Sex, therefore, used for any other purpose than for procreation became immoral, animalistic, and self-defiling. As a result we developed an attitude toward sex which denied the basic fact of our sexuality that our biological sex drive would, one way or another, find some way of expression. But when it did, we became very troubled, guilty, concerned, and anxious. The parade of many guilt-ridden, moralistic parents crowding counseling offices, minister's studies, and psychotherapist's suites is a direct consequence of our being indoctrinated by the "thou shalt not" attitude toward human sexuality.

So what happens, for example, when sexual development occurs and one's sex drive asserts itself? Many men can remember when they had their first penis erection and they became conscious of the erect penis during puberty. What was happening? What does this mean? For many who had received no sex education at all, it had to be bad, it was sinful, because it had something to do with sex. But the first "wet dream" was a real killer. Bad, sinful, dirty. What made it especially troublesome was that it was often accompanied by a sexual dream and "good boys" just don't think about things like that. Furthermore, some of us had mothers who never allowed us a moment of privacy; who discovered by careful scrutiny of the bed linens or our clothing that we had a "wet dream" and made sure that we heard the "proper" lecture on the evils of sex.

Most of us, as we grew up, learned from our friends a few choice sexual words, some of them the four-letter variety, and we used them because we either wanted to impress someone, or we didn't know what they really meant. Almost always the use of a sexually-colored word resulted in a different kind of punishment than the normal slang or swearing words would deserve. Many of us remember either having our mouths washed out with soap and water, or at least we were faced with that threat. Of course our mother wanted to be sure that we didn't use the words again, but in the process she reinforced an attitude that sex is dirty and naughty and that it deserved some extreme form of punishment.

Our parents were embarrassed when we asked them simple little questions about sex. They really didn't know how to answer them because they had not figured it out in their own lives as they too had been brought up on the "thou shalt not" philosophy. This philosophy was not only related to specific behaviors, but also it meant that one was to avoid talking about sex because this would only encourage more bad behavior, and, therefore, everything was hush-hush! We just don't talk about that. The consequence was that we both repressed and suppressed all of our sexual desires and needs. By the time a youngster gets old enough to be told, according to the feelings of the parents, he already knows. It is estimated that at least two-thirds of the boys, for example, who were told about sexual intercouse by their parents, already know about it. They had received their information, frequently misinformation filled with negative emotionalism, from their peers, from bad jokes, and indirectly from observing their parents themselves as they displayed their attitudes in relationship to each other.

As we grew a little older, we began to discover that there was something called a "wifely duty" that women had to fulfill in marriage. This attitude was more common in the past, but it still haunts many marriages. This attitude is two-pronged. On the one hand there is the wife who has learned this attitude and has resigned herself to fulfill this role. Her approach is: "Oh, all right, go ahead, you are just like all men, you have to have it. Please hurry. I have many other more important things to do." Then right in the middle of this great big intense, emotional experience, she says something like this: "Did you put the cat out when you went downstairs, John?" Tragically, many women believe they have to give in to their men and their desires just to keep them from seeking extra-marital affairs. On the other hand, there is the husband who views sexual intercourse as a matter of rights; he forces the wife to submit to his demands in return for which she gains favors and security. The duty-right attitude is cold, one-sided, uninteresting, unromantic, and completely unchallenging as it is composed of the imposition of, and unwilling performance of duty. This idea, in part, is based on an old-fashioned idea that the most important reason for a man marrying is to satisfy his sexual desires in a legal way. Therefore, it becomes almost a religious command for the woman to take care of him.

Attitudes toward pregnancy are also picked up early in our childhood. It was very much a part of our family life, but until we got a little older and found out from the other kids, we really didn't know much about it. It is very possible that pregnancy is where a lot of our myths had their origin. Since years ago there was little that people could do about preventing pregnancy except not to have sexual intercourse, and obviously they did not want the young girls to get pregnant because this would be embarrassing, and besides, the child would not have a father. There was a sort of universal decision that was arrived at and that was to "scare the daylights" out of the girls. This was the *one* way to keep the girl from having sexual intercourse and getting pregnant. This fear conditioning was reinforced by the fear of venereal disease which was discussed in only the most general way and the fear of mental or psychological illness. Of course, these methods really didn't work, but they led to some negative conditioning on the part of the young child.

How this conditioning worked can be seen in a simple and common illustration. One of the things that has happened to many women during their teens is that mother carefully checked their menstruation. They were not really told what they were checking for, but they could expect the subtle question every month. "Did you have your period yet, honey?" And then throwing a fit if she didn't. On the surface we might feel that this is simply good parental concern and responsibility, but when we take a closer look, we discover that this really said something to the girl about sex. It said again and again to the girl that this sex is dirty, fearful, and shameful, and that it's to be done only when you are married, at night, preferably in the dark, and only when you have to have it at that. If one adds to the above some of the other implications of menstruation inherited from the past, we can better understand one of the blocks to an adequate, healthy, sexual response. The two basic concepts from our Mosaic-Christian heritage which prove to be very harmful are the idea of menstruation as a "curse" on womanhood, and the idea of the "uncleanness" and "untouchability" of women during menstruation. Of course, current scientific knowledge gives no support to these ideas which were really only aspects of primitive religious symbolism and ritual.

A masculine myth, maybe one of the most important, which is very destructive for sexual adjustment, is the idea of the male "conquering" women. In our culture, the "big man" around the school, campus, or community, is the one who has been out with all the girls and is always boasting about his conquests. Of course, it may have been as much ego-building through boasting about imagined conquests as the real thing, but the consequences are almost the same. The young man learns that conquering women is the thing to do. This myth is complemented by a companion belief that men really don't have any way of controlling their sexual needs and drives and, therefore, they must relieve their sexual pressures in this way. It is difficult to determine whether this myth is an excuse to exploit or a reason for their behavior. Maybe it is both. Nevertheless, this kind of sexual behavior is a "hurting kind of sex," because it involves taking something from someone else. No matter how the man rationalizes this kind of behavior, it is very destructive. To treat another person as an object, a thing to be used and possibly discarded, a goal to be conquered, is a violation of one's own integrity as well as the other person's. The acceptance of the current playboy jargon of "making," "getting," and "laying" a girl is an expression of an "I-It" relationship which degrades one of God's creations as well as oneself. Part of the reason why in marriage many men find it so hard to love their women is that "big, strong men" don't do that, they simply conquer their women. It is difficult to understand why men cannot be responsible sexually unless one clearly understands their training and background with respect to this attitude toward women.

One of the phoniest, most dishonest beliefs that many men hold is that they know everything that needs to be known about sex. After all, haven't we been discussing the topic among ourselves for years, haven't we shared all those sexy little books, haven't we passed on the latest issue of *Playboy* consistently? So most men have convinced themselves that they know everything and then they proceed to convince their wives of this fact. Of course, no man would ever dare to admit that maybe he doesn't know everything. However, as we make a careful study of the facts, a different picture seems to emerge. Early in marriage most men ejaculate too soon, perhaps the first twenty-five, or would it be more accurate to say the first several hundred times? Is this not a basic dishonesty and false pride? But it does happen and we continue to keep up the pretense of knowledge which makes it difficult for us to learn, discover, or appreciate our partner. Men need to admit that they really don't know much about women, how to approach them or how to treat them, because we really don't know how we ourselves function completely. Therefore, rather than telling our wives they are "frigid" or cold, we need to admit we do not know and begin by asking ourselves honestly why our wives respond to us as they do.

We grow up with a lot of conditioned-in fears about sexual intercourse. One of the most common is the fear of pain. To a large extent the fear of pain comes to us from an earlier period of history when sex was considered a masculine privilege and a feminine duty. This was before the idea of mutuality was considered and it was not uncommon for the man to be very crude and rough in order to prove that his wife was a virgin. Consequently, many girls came to fear their first sexual intercourse. The fear of pain is absolutely unfounded and unnecessary. The medieval sign of blood stains on the bed sheets is archaic and cruel, even sadistic. A brief visit with the family physician during the pre-marital check-up ought to eliminate this as a tension point. A husband who assumes his wife is non-virgin because of the lack of pain or bleeding displays a woeful ignorance about female anatomy and an outdated attitude with respect to the female genital tract.

To further complicate our development of healthy sexual attitudes, is the fact that we have had so many advisors with all kinds of bits and pieces of information which brought sex right down into the gutter, the four-letter-word variety. We have a lot of tavern information coming from dormitories, barracks, peer groups, and a bit from all over. Just about all of the information was bad because it was given by those who knew so little about sex and had so little sexual satisfaction that they had to talk about it all of the time. This is how they got their "kicks." "Confusion begets more confusion," is a statement that is extremely valid as it is applied to sexual knowledge. Bad information is little better than no information and sometimes worse. A great deal of our problem results from misinformation and no information. This manifests itself in neurotic repression and inhibition of normal sexual expression. There is little doubt that the guilt, shame, unrealistic demands, and expectations in the realm of sex cause problems because they bring distortion and a distorted approach and interest to a very normal human need. We also often turn to the mass media with its nudity, girlie magazines, seductive females, adult-only labels, and suggestive perversion, for our knowledge as well as to satisfy our neurotic anxieties. We face a paradox in our society and that is the fact that we live in a period of time in which illicit sex is severely condemned by society in general, while on the other hand illicit sex is made enticing and desirable by the hucksters of advertising.

Several examples, from a list of many, will illustrate the problems or misinformation gleaned from poor sources. One of the things taught in male peer groups is that "deep penetration" is a tremendously important thing to accomplish in the sexual act and that this brings tremendous satisfaction to the wife as it brings her to her climax. You really have to "send" these gals by penetrating deeply. What are the facts about this myth? First of all, deep penetration is totally unnecessary because of her anatomical make-up. She has no nerve endings inside to be sensitive to either size or depth of the penetration. Her sensitive organs are the vulva, clitoris, and her breasts and they are important in the response she makes or is able to make. It is movement and the feeling of love, heightened by the intensity of physical and emotional feeling that brings her to a climax and she could care less at this particular moment about the size of the penis or the depth of the penetration.

Secondly, deep penetration rather than aiding the wife to climax actually can hurt a woman and physically harm her. All that one needs to do to understand why is to look at a cross-sectional drawing of the female anatomy. Finally, with deep penetration, as gleaned from the "dirty little jokes and books," the man raises the woman up to get this deep penetration. What happens when the woman is raised? If she is on her back, as most men seem to prefer, she is in a poor position in the first place for most people and when the man tries to penetrate deeply and raises her up, he actually withdraws contact from the two most sensitive areas of her body, the breasts and the clitoris. So rather than helping her achieve her climax, she may actually cool off during this attempt at deep penetration.

Closely related to the idea of "deep penetration" is the belief held by many men, especially early in marriage, that they need to prove their masculinity by an aggressive display of potency and virility. Some men feel that it is their task to initiate their wife into the sexual experience as rapidly as possible and they wish to do this as soon as possible to satisfy their own sexual desires and needs. Consequently haste, crudeness, roughness, selfishness, and thoughtlessness become self-defeating because they inhibit the response of the woman making it all the more necessary, psychologically, for the man to attempt to prove his potency and virility. The harder he tries the less successful he becomes, and the more anxious and insecure he feels. In the final analysis, there is no need to prove either because nature has endowed all men with these qualities. The greatest sense of pride a man may achieve sexually is that he has been able to give his wife satisfaction and happiness which come only through love, understanding, consideration and cooperation.

A great deal of our information on sex comes from professionals and marriage manuals. A lot of medical people, and related professionals, are basically out to make the "fast buck" from selling books on sexual techniques. Unfortunately, most of the authors of these materials say nothing about the person or communication, but simply talk about the techniques of sex. One of the nonsensical approaches usually includes a discussion, and in some cases illustrations, of the "forty-six positions of ecstasy in sexual intercourse." It does sell books. However, position makes little difference because sexual intercourse is what he is and what she is, and how each treats the other, and not what specific method is used. No one position is "normal" or more acceptable than another. There are many positions, variations of them, and variations upon the variations. Experimentation is important in achieving sexual fulfillment when based on the needs and desires of the couple. The major problem the couple needs to be concerned about is to avoid an exaggerated concern for the "how," or their sexual relationships may become artificial, restrained, and unsatisfying. Freedom and spontaneity need to be preserved. It is not "the position" which is important but a position or positions that best meet the needs of the couple; and this the couple will need to find out together as they communicate totally their needs to each other and then seek to meet them.

Our final consideration in this chapter is a discussion of the fact that male and female were created as two entirely different people. The discussion will be limited to recognizing their differences as they relate to the sexual sphere of human behavior. We will need to recognize at the onset that not all the differences are biological. Some may be culturally determined. However, they are very important because they have been given various meanings by our culture and we have learned to attach these meanings to differences, expectations, and prohibitions. The following diagram will introduce in a visual way the major concept we will be discussing:

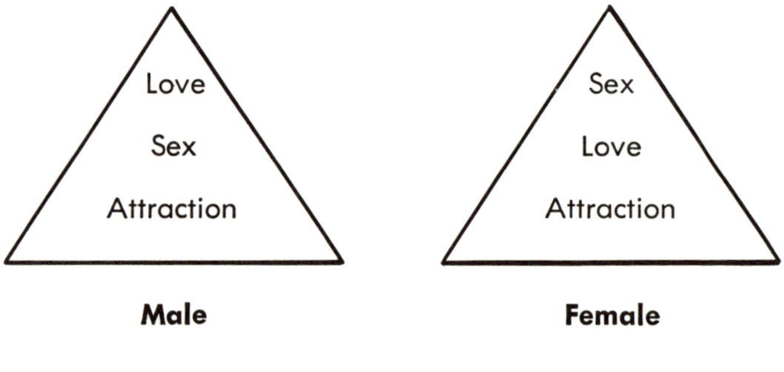

As you can see, the diagram is composed of only three words: *attraction, love* and *sex.* One pyramid model represents the male, the other the female. The words are arranged in an entirely different order, except for the word "attraction" which men and women have in common. Marriages have this in common. We recognize and observe very clearly that the male is attracted very strongly to the female. Up from the face of the pyramid, after "attraction," we placed the word "sex," implying that the male moves from "attraction" to "sex." And finally, as sexual maturity develops in the male, and usually only then, does he reach a totally mature "love." Possibly more women need to consider this diagram with concern. One of the often-heard complaints in the counselor's office is that "I think my husband is a sex fiend." Is he really, or how can we explain this apparent behavior? Can't this statement be made generally about most good, red-blooded, American boys? He is sex-oriented and he builds his love through sex. Sex is all important. How he functions sexually determines how he feels about himself, and in reverse, how he feels about himself determines how he functions sexually. Every male wants to function adequately in the sexual aspect of marriage. Every male wants to bring satisfaction to his wife through the sexual relationship. If he does he is confident, he feels strong within himself, he feels very masculine, and then he reaches the maturity that he needs to grow into a mature type of love.

The female is a different type of person. Although she begins with "attraction," her next move is to "love," not to "sex." What she desires most of all in marriage is love. This is what she wants from her children and from her husband. She wants and needs love. Sex she wants too, but for the female, sex is a by-product or self-fulfillment of love in the sense that she must first have love before she can reach a totally complete mature sexuality.

This is the "American sexual dilemma." This is the source of almost all the problems in the sexual area that come to the attention of counselors. The dilemma is basically the failure to understand that the female must have love to reach sexual maturity and that the male must have sex to reach a maturity in love.

What do we mean when we say that the woman needs love? She really needs many things. She needs attention from her husband; she needs a real show of affection and it has to say clearly: "I love you." The big, masculine, American male often says: "Why should I have to tell her that I love her? I married her, didn't I? She should know that I love her. I bought her a house to live in. I provide her with a good wardrobe. I bought her new furniture. She has everything that she needs. Besides, I take her on vacations, etc., etc." This is not really what a woman needs; this is not what she really wants the most; this is but a display of external affection which does not alone satisfy her. Rather, she wants to be loved and told that she is loved; she wants to be shown that she is loved; she wants to be held, caressed, and fondled in a loving sort of way. These are important to a woman. She also wants to be respected as a person, especially by her husband, to be treated as a person, to feel a part of his life, and feel needed by her husband. Finally, every woman wants some strength in her man. She wants him to be as strong or stronger than she is. A woman wants to look up to a man who is strong in the home. And only when she receives all of these things to some degree, and many more little things that go with and into the expression of love, can she respond in a mature fashion sexually. Males need to have a clearer understanding of the fact that this is the way females function. The cry of males heard much too often is: "If you love me, you will respond, you will be as ready for sexual activity as I am." This, of course, is not true because in American society not only is a woman not ready, she cannot be made ready unless she has love from her husband and knows it. Then she can respond eventually — totally — sexually. Anything less robs the woman of her potential which in turn robs the man of his.

Why does the American male fail to help his wife achieve adequate sexual maturity? Mostly it comes from his conditioning and experience. Marie Robinson, one of our outstanding modern psychiatrists, says that fifty percent of our married women suffer from frigidity and that of this fifty percent less than one percent are actually frigid. The rest are simply mistreated by their husbands. How are they mistreated? How does the normal courtship-engagement-marriage go? There is no doubt about the fact that the young male knows what a young woman needs. All day long, every time he sees her, it's: "I love you; you are pretty; you have adorable hair; I would like to spend the rest of my life with you. We will sit by the fireside together, etc." He paints a beautiful picture of continuing love that meets a woman's needs exactly. One might say that when he is trying to get her into bed for the first time, he functions very adequately.

Now comes the wedding. He hurries off to buy the license, he comes home, they get married, he holds up the license and says: "I'm sure glad this is over. I don't have to do any of this stuff any more." And from this day forward an awful lot of women in the United States never again hear the words: "I love you." Why not? Simply because men in our society are conditioned not to be emotional after marriage. This is a feminine trait and not masculine behavior. Furthermore, if this woman were mature, according to the man's belief, "she would know that I love her and this would be all there is to it."

We need to get back to a clear recognition of these basic concepts before we can think about making sex work in marriage. It cannot be done through a trial and error system and we simply cannot force it to work. We bring all kinds of things into marriage and it isn't any wonder that we spend years of friction and struggle just trying to solve this sexual thing. A woman who has been brought up on the idea that sex is dirty (and if she doesn't leave this feeling at the altar), requires years and years of patient concern on her husband's part to help her relax enough to thoroughly enjoy herself sexually. Consider the man who has been brought up to believe he knows everything that needs to be known about sex, how can he sit down with his wife and say: "No, honey, I can't stand this thing, I am frustrating you every time. There must be something wrong. What is it?" This will be extremely difficult because he has been conditioned and trained that a man does not admit there is anything wrong.

Still it is completely necessary that we face each other and talk these things over honestly. Because what is sex really? It is not anything sinful. It is something beautiful. As one considers sex, one should be able to see God's continuing creation. God creates us, we marry, then we keep on with this creation the rest of our lives. God created love and this is what we recreate in marriage. We do not just create children, but people who know how to love one another. It is through this beautiful act of sexual intercourse that we help to create, broaden, and deepen the love that we already have for each other.

It only makes good sense for all of us to spend a lot of time honestly discussing our feelings about sex and to talk through our feelings. We must rid ourselves of the factors which we take to bed with us that harm our relationships so that we can go to bed with some joy and with some reasonable expectations.

For Summary and Review

1. Most of us suffer in our sexual experience because we come from a conservative, puritanical background that gave us a great deal of misinformation. List specifically the major thoughts and concepts about sex most of us grew up with.
2. How free were the members of your family to bring up matters of sex? What factors affected freedom — or the lack of it?

3. Several myths that are supposedly essential to successful sexual intercourse were discussed. List and discuss briefly others that play a role in the hurting kind of sexuality.
4. Write a definition of "sexuality" as you understand it. Check with several other persons. How do the definitions differ? In what respects were they similar?
5. Why didn't God create us as "neuter" rather than male and female?
6. God said "it is good" after he created MAN. What is your interpretation (after a little thought and research) of this statement?
7. Any suggestions on how to improve the discussion would be appreciated.

Chapter 8

The Total Climax of Love

THE TOTAL CLIMAX OF love is a beautiful concept to understand. It is something almost all couples can achieve to a much higher level than is now being accomplished. It is necessary for all couples to work on their love-making every day so that better and more loving people will go to bed at night. People make love and these two people have to be prepared through a lifetime of living. In a sense, the only two people who can "really" make love are real Christians who live as Christ suggested that they live. The penis and vagina do not make love, it is two people who make love to each other. Therefore, it is not technique, it is not method, it is not what one pushes or presses that is important, but instead, who the persons are. Since all persons have varying sexual needs and responses because they are different persons, the goal of this chapter is to help the reader to begin thinking about what to do and how to do it in his home. The only way that the reader can successfully accomplish this is through honest communication and love in his marriage.

The beautiful, simultaneous climax that presumably occurs every time two people have intercourse has been built up and romanticized in this country into something wonderful – but it is largely unrealistic. The simultaneous climax designed by God, is, however, a beautiful thing in itself. The union of two well-adjusted people in a marriage under God's plan with His intentions and with His full consent is a beautiful thing. A truly Christian couple have the potential to go beyond simply a physical simultaneous climax; that is a total offering of love to each other and through the growth of love in the sexual climax with each other, to move in depth to a complete kind of love, patterned after a Divine love. To achieve what we will call a total climax of the two personalities, the total climax of love, the physical simultaneous climax being an important part, the man and the woman have to be totally prepared. By using the word "totally" we may be idealizing because it is something we will not always achieve. But it can serve well as a goal toward which the couple can strive as they build a life together in marriage.

All couples need total preparation on three separate but closely related levels: emotional, spiritual, and physical. The physical is perhaps the least important of the three levels and probably the least complex to understand, but it is a level that cannot be ignored.

How do we prepare each other emotionally? Someone has stated a perceptive truism: "If you want to make out with a woman at night, you better start loving her in the morning." One fact men often fail to understand in their knowledge about women is the fact that most women cannot respond with a mature sexuality unless they first feel a mature love being offered by the man which includes plain, common, decent, human treatment all day long. You treat her like a lady all day long and like someone you respect and like someone whom you love.

Probably a large percentage of the marital problems in this country center directly around the feelings of the male that he is sexually deprived. He often complains bitterly about this, especially to himself. He feels very sorry for himself. What is the basic reason for this felt problem? The answer is not difficult because in most cases it is simply because he is not giving enough, not meeting his wife's needs. She needs affection, and lots of it, and it has to be for real. She has to know that she is loved and too often the only way she can discover this fact is for him to tell her verbally. Women need attention; they need to feel as though they are important to men; they need someone to listen to them, to consider what they say, and to respect them for what they are. They need someone to look up to them as well as someone to look up to. Women need to feel important. If women feel secure as a result of having these feelings they feel strength in themselves and confidence in their femininity. It is just this strength and confidence that the male needs to respond adequately sexually.

How does this operate in actual experience? As we have discussed earlier, many females are sure they married a real sex fiend. In quite a real sense the wife likely has created a man who responds to her in the way he feels he must and she, therefore, has got the guy all hung up on sex. He thinks about sex almost constantly. As she defends herself from the guy, afraid that if she gives him the least little bit of encouragement he will want to go right to bed, she knocks him down and rejects his approaches. Sigmund Freud suggested that in an abstract way she "castrates" the male. So often the insecure woman criticizes her husband all day long, even sexually. She cuts him down, verbally chops him up, and then she wonders why he isn't her great big, strong hunk of a man. The obvious reason is that she hasn't built such a man. The woman needs to be aware of a physical fact of the male sexual anatomy and drive to be able to adjust maturely and constructively in a sexual sense. If she only gives it enough time his drive tends to reduce as hers becomes awakened and more intense; ultimately they will merge as sexual mutuality is developed. Moreover, by resisting, criticizing and denying the male's expression of his sexual need she actually increases his need for expression. A man also needs praise, respect, and strength and when it is absent he feels insecure and incomplete. Consequently, he feels a need to prove himself a complete and successful man. His ego is much more involved in his successful performance of his sex role than is found in the woman. If the woman is fully aware of this and is honest enough to tell him how she feels, and the two are willing to learn and grow together, he will no longer feel the need to "prove" himself and sex will become a mutually satisfying and fulfilling experience.

It is important to remember that sex is also a spiritual act and not just an emotional, physical kind of thing, because it involves, in a harmonious, complimentary way, body, mind and soul. In some cases many American women would like to make it completely spiritual so that instead of getting into bed and making love with their husbands, they would rather kneel down alongside the bed and pray for love. This would be easier because they would be receiving and would not have to be involved in giving. However, our emphasis at this point is not so much on prayer as it is on the idea that God created sex in beauty and bestowed upon it dignity with a tremendous potential for building and keeping love in the home. Sex in order to reach the potential possible must be surrounded with dignity and love.

How is dignity violated in many marriages? One example might be found in a brief analogy. A recently married girl came into the counseling office and her story may describe the plight of many women in this same situation. She was a virgin at marriage and plenty afraid of sex. On their wedding day her husband, a bit unsure of himself, wanted to prove his masculinity and proceeded to get drunk. They went to a motel in the same town and began to make love. As one thinks about the spiritual components of this kind of love-making it is easy to understand what happened in this marriage. She was afraid to begin with. This drunken male came in and literally attacked her. All the fears that she had all of her life and that were right on the surface were all confirmed. This is what she expected it to be and she was afraid. For the rest of her life she will remember this honeymoon experience and consciously or unconsciously she will respond to him every time he makes an approach to her based on the experience.

Sex based on the kind of urgency that alcohol often produces can be likened more to "rape" than love. Sexual intercourse can become a completely disgusting situation when the man demands and forces his need for relief on his wife. To many, alcohol becomes a great deceiver. Men under its influence usually think they are tremendous lovers, but it's all in their heads. No woman gets much pleasure from sex when she is breathing alcohol fumes and when he is not performing adequately. This destroys the spiritual dignity of the act. Therefore, each partner needs to be constantly evaluating their relationship with each other and ask, "Are we making our sexual relationship a beautiful thing or are we destroying its dignity by using alcohol or by making it a duty or simply making it a dull, boring routine?"

Spiritual preparation, finally, brings about a strong conviction and belief in the beauty of the sex act because it is an important part of God's creation. To achieve the ideal of total climax or total union, sex must be disassociated from the sense of wrong and sin. Each must come to realize that there can be no wrong or sin in this beautiful act God originated for men to achieve perfection of love in marriage.

Physically we prepare each other the best by doing what comes naturally. It appears that the biggest problem for many of us is to work through the many inhibitions so that we are free to respond naturally. In most women, the breasts are especially sensitive; the clitoris which lies at the top of the vagina in most women contains very sensitive nerve endings. In most women the clitoris is her sexual trigger, just as the breasts and kissing may be. Naturally and normally a man desires to caress, fondle, and enjoy the breasts; he desires to caress, fondle, and enjoy the vagina. This is significant because, as he does so, he prepares the woman in the way she needs and should be prepared. This seems simple and natural enough, so what's the problem?

Several problems are evident. *First,* there are so many taboos against natural expression of sexual love and concern. There are taboos with respect to modesty such as seeing and touching, bodily contacts, such as mouth-genital foreplay and aggressiveness and passiveness, to name a few restrictions on spontaneous responses. *Secondly,* incomplete knowledge about the importance and meaning of sex, as well as about male and female anatomy, encourages an urgency that will usually leave sex needs, especially the female's, unmet, unfulfilled and often frustrated. Patience and understanding become very important in one's sexual relationship with his spouse.

If spontaneity, natural responses, and patience are practiced during the physical preparation, two important things happen. *First,* the female becomes completely lubricated and this is essential. Sometimes very good use can be made of commercial lubrication jellies and salves; however, usually these will not be necessary if the female is properly prepared through foreplay. *Secondly,* she will ultimately reach the point where she desires and needs the penis inserted. At this point the penis can be inserted with a minimum of pressure and the ejaculation can be delayed with less urgency. Since men tend to be very unreliable, it makes good sense to adequately prepare the woman so that both can respond in a more complete way. In former periods of history, this may not have been crucial because women had much lower expectations from sex, generally. Today, however, most literate women know about what can potentially be experienced and the male needs to know how to make this expectation a reality. It is not difficult when he approaches sex with a desire to learn and understand; with the closed-mind approach it may well be nigh impossible for the total climax of love to occur. As the male becomes increasingly aware of his partner's sensitive, "trigger" areas, he learns how to enhance, control, slow up, or speed up, her responses so that the two may find complete union together. Much good common sense goes a long way in mutual sex adjustment.

There are some concerns for the female in the physical preparations of the male which need some open discussion. Basically, most of the physical preparation of the man is an emotional one. If he has some confidence in himself, if he doesn't have to prove his virility or potency, if he knows his partner respects and loves him it becomes much easier for him to relax and control his ejaculation and wait for his wife's climax. Note that the reference was for it to become easier and not automatically make possible complete control. The male needs consciously to develop the ability to hold back the ejaculation because it does not just happen. Physically the wife can help the male by fondling, caressing or playing with the penis and testicles. This arousal of the male will result in a small loss of fluid which reduces the pressure and urgency. This permits the male to hold back as he continues to meet his partner's needs. This comes naturally as both seek to thoroughly love and enjoy each other in this way. For the female as well as the male it requires adequate knowledge of the anatomy as well as open, frank, and honest communication about these normal needs.

Probably, sexual frustration is a common thing that occurs constantly in a lot of marriages. Consequently, the way we react to frustration is the most important issue. So what? What are we trying for? Are we trying to prove something in the marriage? Or are we just trying to love each other? If we are trying to love each other and if the wife doesn't immediately have this big orgasm every time, or if the husband doesn't, what's the difference? If the man ejaculates too soon, all that he needs to do is to keep on loving his wife and eventually she will have an orgasm. It may not be the "great big bang" the marriage manuals say it should be, but she will have an orgasm that will leave her satisfied and she will have a feeling of being loved. Perhaps, she will be much more satisfied than if she had had the ultimate, because she knows that he has kept on loving her and that he cares. The total climax of love is something we need to keep working for because there is no need to settle for anything less. If one seeks to reach a perfection in love, it makes each subsequent experience better. The way partners work this out is their decision. There can be no routine, pattern, method, or position which can be universally applied; rather each couple through knowledge, understanding love and concern make their own marriage bed which meets their own needs.

To conclude our discussion on mature sexual adjustment contained in the last three chapters, it is necessary to pull together a few loose ends and concepts affecting sexual adjustment.

One concept which needs some attention today is how to view the sexually aggressive woman. As women have become more educated, more liberated from restraining traditional stereotypes, this has become a matter of concern. Probably the most difficult aspect for the male is that he is taught not to expect this from his wife. He is enculturated with the idea that "good" girls don't behave this way, or that if she is aggressive sexually that she is "over-sexed." The traditional sexual role for the woman was to be passive, even though the idea is found more in folklore than in reality. As a result of this conditioning the male often reacts negatively to the female's assertion of her sexuality in an aggressive manner. Directly related to the new assertion of aggressiveness on the part of the female is the male "flight" from sex; i.e., he avoids sex, he tries to escape entanglement and he often becomes impotent as a consequence. This is a relatively new problem and needs to be faced honestly because it affects an increasing number of males.

There is no logical, rational, or adequate reason, biologically, psychologically, ethically, or otherwise, why a woman should not take an active, aggressive part in a couple's loveplay and sexual intercourse itself, even going so far as taking the initiative. Rather men should feel gratified that their partners are so sexually aroused that their needs and desires are so nearly parallel their own. Instead of interfering with the sexual adjustment, increasing female aggression should make adequate sexual adjustment much easier over a shorter period of time. Man should not attempt to escape from it but utilize the behavior and be grateful. The answers to the needs of both the sexually aggressive female and the under-aggressive male are exactly the same. Both are caused by feelings of inadequacy and insecurity, therefore, both need reassurance, confidence, support and love.

There are a number of final thoughts that we should consider before leaving this area of sex adjustment. All of the concepts which follow either directly or indirectly affect the possibility of achieving the total climax of love. The first concept we need to look at is consideration for each other; it is a need we frequently forget. For example, a woman is frequently tired, she is home all day with several small children; she is very busy, she has many chores to do. There are many times she is legitimately tired. The husband needs to be considerate at such a time. We need, however, to add that marriage counselors hear too many accounts of tiredness that have nothing to do with physical fatigue. Instead, feigned tiredness is an escape mechanism used to avoid sex. Many women are tired too many nights out of the year. Women need to evaluate this response carefully to try to determine if it is in fact physical tiredness or a conscious or unconscious attempt to withhold sex from one's partner. If it is the latter, why? Is sex the focal point of tension? Or is it a reflection of conflicts in other areas which has led to avoidance, resistance, and withholding?

There are times of special tensions when consideration is most important and men generally forget. One of these times is during pregnancy. During pregnancy the woman experiences many different feelings and moods. No two women react the same but many women become very emotional, and are usually high-strung. During pregnancy the woman needs a lot of non-sexual attention and love; much more than she usually does. Many also need much more sexual love during this time but this would vary considerably. There is no reason, except for specific cases, that normal sexual relations should not continue until at least six months into the pregnancy. Care and concern must be exercised and advice from the family doctor plus good communication can make this period a very satisfying time sexually.

Pre-menstrual tensions are quite common. As a matter of fact, probably every woman has some sort of pre-menstrual tension. The tensions can be very evident when some kind of birth control is practiced. Even discarding the fear of pregnancy, most women experience some periodicity in their emotional feelings. Men need to be observing and conscious of the rapid changes in moods that occur and then adjust their behavior to meet the woman's particular needs at this time. Her periodicity may manifest itself in a heightened desire for sex or a decreasing desire. The man can learn to appreciate and respect her desires and needs only through conscious effort. No one can furnish him with information about his wife, except the wife herself. She need not hesitate to communicate her feelings to him either directly or through the use of many indirect and subtle means.

The change of life or menopause can be a disastrous time in some homes. Almost everyone has heard the old wives' tales about sex life ending with the change of life. Unfortunately, the concern and fear begin long before menopause actually has taken place. Every normal woman will experience rather drastic bodily changes that tend to leave her rather upset during the change of life. But these are small compared to the psychological fears experienced by the woman who has been frustrated during her life. Most research shows that a woman's sexual desire ordinarily continues undiminished until she is over sixty years of age and for the male even longer. This is clearly long after menopause and clearly indicates that ordinarily no physical reasons exist for a woman's sex life to end. Nor does a hysterectomy or the removal of ovaries, which is not unusual during this period, diminish the sex drive or prevent its complete satisfaction. The crucial factors are one's attitudes toward sex and one's emotional stability. Really, if one considers the potential of sex fulfillment, it is enhanced by menopause because fear of pregnancy is now removed and more complete expression and satisfaction are possible. Generally, the better the mental health before menopause, the fewer unpleasant symptoms the woman will have when it occurs. It becomes imperative then that both husband and wife strive diligently to work out their adjustments early in marriage so that these strengths help offset the negative potentials of menopause.

Physical cleanliness in marriage is another very important consideration in marriage sexual adjustment. During the courtship days one could hardly be clean enough, dress well enough, etc. but after marriage there is often a tendency to let down. Old jeans, messy hair, and sloppy habits result in a corresponding lack of compliments. Why? He is not a liar; he doesn't know what to say. Then there are the men who do not shave on weekends, or who only shave on the weekend; who never dress up to take their wives out; who physically are not clean about themselves. This complaint from women comes so often in counseling that it is necessary to consider. Since sexual relations are intimate, anything that destroys them should be eliminated. Personal hygiene for both partners enhances the enjoyment of the most intimate of relationships.

Privacy is a very real need for most people. Privacy may not always be easy to secure. The observing eyes or hearing ears of neighbors, relatives, and children can be very destructive as they make it impossible for the partners to totally give and respond to each other sexually.

Finally, we need to make the bedroom a place of love so that our sex life will be more beautiful and far more effective. Too often sex and sin have gone hand in hand. We have lived by negatives: "Don't do this! Don't do that! Don't do something else! This is a sin! This is wrong!" The result has been that most of us go to bed with a guilty or uneasy conscience. Religiously, this is really not true at all, we have only assumed such to be so. The Bible itself declares sex to be sacred and beautiful, even to the extent that Christ's relationship to the Church is compared with human sexuality.

Sin, therefore, is an extremely difficult thing to commit by a married couple in the privacy and intimacy of their bedroom. We are simply loving each other as God intended us to do (Mutuality, see 1 Corinthians 7:3-5; 11:3-5).

For Summary and Review

1. Discuss: "Sexual intercourse is not the climax of technique, as so many today seem to think. But rather, it is the climax of the love-relationship itself."
2. Discuss: The total climax of love is an outgrowth of everything we are all day long.
3. What do you personally believe should be the potential of sex in marriage? What will the couple need to do to realize this potential?
4. What does the man/woman need to know about the woman/man in order to adequately fulfill the needs of the woman/man?
5. What significant facts does the diagram in Chapter 7 when applied to this chapter identify? How does the lack in the understanding of these relationships contribute to many of the stereotypes commonly referred to in male-female relationships?
6. Analyze the following statements:
    a. "If I were a woman and I wanted to keep my husband, I would see to it that he were loved and loved sexually."
    b. "If you want to make out with your wife in the evening, then you had better start loving her in the morning."
7. Are there any significant concepts that you feel are missing in this chapter?

Chapter 9

Plan Ahead: Some Thoughts on Contraception

CONCEPTION AND THE BIRTH of new humans is the most commonplace miracle on earth. This brings joy to millions of parents yearly as well as disappointment, frustration and tensions for many. Since humanity is now counted in the billions, the threat of widescale starvation in some areas of the world brings an additional dimension and moral crisis. What is man's role and responsibility? All individuals are involved in the effort to answer this important question, both privately and publicly, whether consciously aware of the issues or not. In this chapter, we shall attempt to discuss the major aspects of one important part of the larger question, that is, responsible family planning. The chapter is not an attempt to persuade the reader to use contraceptives, but rather to evaluate the approaches people are using and identifying the positive, negative, and problem aspects we all need to be aware of in order to make satisfactory rational decisions.

Today families in all walks of life and of every religious and national background practice some form of birth control with varying degrees of success. It is used to limit family size, to space the arrival of children, and to bring a more free, spontaneous and harmonious sexual relationship within marriage. Many well-documented studies indicate that more than ninety out of one hundred couples are practicing some form of birth control and the number is increasing steadily. Therefore, it appears that the traditional question of: "Should we use contraceptives?" has been replaced in actual practice by: "What methods should we use?" This is indeed a very important question because it does involve religious beliefs, social conditioning, aesthetics, individual preference, physical and emotional health, predictive effectiveness, and ease and expense of use. Consequently, the decision should be made after careful and complete consideration so that the method or technique which is chosen is the best for the particular couple involved. What is good for one couple may not be good or appropriate for another. What works and is comfortable and safe for one couple may be uncomfortable and unsafe for another. No method is any better, or predictable, than the couple using it. No couple can safely use any method of contraception without first availing themselves of professional advice and counsel. For many, this could involve medical, clergical, and social counseling because contraception does not just involve what one does, but who one is as a person. Meanings are just as important as the methods and techniques or devices and must be part of the decision-making process if contraception is to adequately accomplish the goal of the couple.

Why are so many couples practicing contraception today? I would like to summarize for you some of the basic reasons so that we will be able to look at the various methods more objectively. Certainly, the changes in birth control practices are part of the sexual revolution we are experiencing in the world today. Involved is a changed concept of sex satisfaction which has moved from male monopoly to sexual mutuality. Traditionally, for a woman to enjoy sex was almost sinful. But today we know, because of the mountain of scientific evidence, that a woman needs to, can, and has the right to enjoy sex with her husband and that she can be active, responsive, and fulfilled in her sex relationship. This healthy new attitude has been of tremendous value to the individual, marriage, and society.

Sexual adjustment of the couple in marriage can at best be achieved only partially if the fear of an unwanted pregnancy is always present during the sexual act. If this fear is removed, the possibility of complete and mutual sex fulfillment is more likely to be achieved and continued by the couple. The meaning of sexual intercouse then is transformed into a beautiful, happy, relaxed, fulfilling experience for both. Sex gives to the marriage strength and radiance not otherwise possible.

Another objective reason for using contraceptives would include: the physical welfare of the mother. If pregnancy occurs during certain periods of physical illness, or mental illness, the consequences for the mother could be very severe, not only for the mother, but for the family in general. Another reason: certain hereditary diseases or characteristics, if passed on to the children would create physical or mental abnormalities. This can be prevented through the use of contraception. Again, the economic situation of the family may be such that adding another child could create undue strains and affect the entire family adversely. Age of the couple could be a significant consideration to be made, especially when compounded with poor health of the mother or economic strains. Goals parents seek for their children are also important factors in determining family size. The above reasons could be expanded and added onto. The major concept is clear, however, that both subjective and objective reasons are involved in the decisions about birth control. Usually a combination of both are involved in the couple's decision.

We will begin our discussion of how married women control pregnancy by an analysis of the "rhythm method." This method is accepted by all religious groups and specifically sanctioned by some. The RM is based on the fact that a woman can conceive only within twenty-four hours after ovulation. Ovulation usually occurs from twelve to sixteen days after the beginning of each menstrual cycle. A normal woman usually discharges her egg in this routine cycle. Unfortunately, we have no certain way of knowing when a woman is about to ovulate or is ovulating. We have estimates on which to calculate, but the calculations can be only a little more reliable than an educated guess. Therefore, even if the couple refrains from sexual intercourse for five days preceding and the four days following the calculated ovulation to allow for safety, it may not at all guarantee that the balance of the cycle is the safe period. Many factors contribute to an irregular schedule or cycle. The way the woman's organs function, illness, anxiety, tiredness and tension all can cause irregularity in both the menstrual cycle and ovulation. Consequently, when the RM is not exactly determined and supervised and carefully followed by the couple, and if the individuals are not temperamentally fitted for it, or if they are only superficially knowledgeable about it, the results can be tragically uncertain and disastrous for them.

Urban G. Steinmetz, from the Upper Penninsula Family Enrichment Bureau, and a family counselor, made a survey of Catholic couples who had chosen the RM. The results were consistent and clear. In fact he could even predict as to what sort of response he would get in an interview. The process usually went something like the following. At the initial interview, Jane Doe comes into the office and sits down. The conversation centers around the fact that Jane has four little children and she wants to know what she can do about this. She is asked: "Did you try the RM?" She replies: "You bet I did and look at all the kids I have." She goes on: "It just doesn't work and my doctor says it doesn't work." The second interview doesn't change many facts, but the third interview is marked by some changes. She becomes a bit more honest and she explains that the reason the RM hasn't worked so well in their home is that they cheated a little. Of course, cheating a little on the RM has the disastrous effect of getting the woman pregnant. So, really, it is not the method but the persons involved which is the most important.

One major concern in the RM is the nine to thirteen days of complete abstinence from sexual intercourse. Is this a realistic expectation? What impact does this have on the needs, expectations and mutual sex adjustment of the couple?

There are of course many rationalizations, most of which are more easily verbalized than practiced. Obviously it does not hurt anyone physically to abstain from sex for a period of time. Certainly, theoretically one should be able to control his or her sexual impulses. Definitely, sex after periods of abstinence can be very exciting and pleasurable. Moreover, if they love each other, they will be willing to wait. All of the above are "good" rationalizations, but not always realistic because two people are involved in the reality of living together in marriage with someone they love and they are affected by various stimuli and situations.

One of the factors often over-stressed is the concept of "self-sacrifice" of the couple during the unsafe period. Can this concept be positive or is it often destructive to the sex adjustment of the couple? Probably it would be helpful to illustrate what too often happens by pulling together some facts which are found in marriage counseling.

Often we find the situation where the man feels he is making a tremendous self-sacrifice and the woman is doing what she wanted to do anyway, going to sleep. She is feeling very noble, he is feeling very hurt. Mutual self-sacrifice is seldom found and, consequently, it breaks down in most homes where it is used as the rationalization. So in many homes, after they have gone through the regular menstrual cycle and dad has behaved himself for five to seven days, he spends a good deal of time thinking about sex. It has aroused him, he is overcharged and ready to go. In fact, he is too ready to go. The first night they do have sexual intercourse, he is too fast, he ejaculates too easily, too soon. This is a very normal biological response for most men after periods of abstinence. He frustrates his wife. She becomes upset about this and she makes a decision in regard to sex. "The next time we have sexual intercourse is going to be the year that Christmas and New Years fall on the same day." The following nights when he makes an approach, she resists and complains of a headache, a cold, her sinuses, or some other ailment. Finally, after several nights, they pass into the unsafe period and two basic things have happened. First of all, dad has moved to the point where sex is a very vital need. The sexual urge is strong and he wants it right now. At this point he uses all the tricks he has learned and he becomes a very persuasive individual. Secondly, something has happened to the woman too. After all, she does love this guy and she has sexual needs also. She recognizes the importance of sex to him and she feels a sense of guilt for denying him sex for so long. So on this particular night, say about the eleventh or twelfth day, all of these things come to a head and they decide mutually that they couldn't be that unlucky. They go to bed and totally enjoy each other. And another RM baby is born. This pattern is consistent, only the specific circumstances are different. It happens because of constant sexual frustration and sexual misunderstanding.

The RM will work within the biological limitations for a couple "if" (and it is a big "if") the sexual relationship is good during the safe period of the cycle, in other words, if the man has enough sex relationships that are satisfying to him. We need to remember that in our earlier discussion on sexual adjustment we said that no sexual relationship can be satisfying to the man unless it also is satisfying to the woman. If the couple matures sexually enough to learn to enjoy each other fully sexually during the safe period of the cycle, the unsafe period will be no great problem. But the feelings and attitudes must be mutual. If we expect the man to make the large sacrifices, the wife must insure that he receives all the sexual satisfaction he needs during the safe period, and this is something she really should enjoy doing anyway.

The RM does provide the aesthetic beauty of natural intercourse that cannot be achieved through the use of some mechanical devices. However, human sexual desires and needs for each other cannot be regulated by clocks or calendars, or by the fact that it is the wrong time of the month. Therefore, spontaneity of sexual expression can be lost when the RM is used by the couple.

Couples desiring to use the RM with maximal hope of success, should consult with the family physician who can help them to determine the safe and unsafe days. There is hope for improvement in the method of determination of the safe days as newer and more simple procedures for pin-pointing the ovulation are discovered. Even now, the RM is far more effective than no contraceptives at all. Couples who have no religious or moral beliefs opposing the use of other contraceptives but still desire to use the RM could well use one or several of the other available devices if they engage in sexual intercourse during the unsafe period. Your family physician would be able to provide you with specific information as to what to use to maximize protection from pregnancy.

One of the oldest means of pregnancy prevention is coitus interruptus, or withdrawal of the penis before ejaculation. Thus the semen is deposited outside the genital tract. Not only is this technique one of the oldest, but it is probably very widespread in its use today. Its reliability is open to very serious question because of the very nature of sexual intercourse and the biological make-up of the male. In the first place, the man may not withdraw in time. It is a fact that for most men, at least early in their sexual life, at the time they have orgasm and ejaculate they desire the deepest penetration of the penis into the vagina. Therefore, they are expected to perform a voluntary rational act at a time when they are most likely to be motivated by an involuntary, irrational impulse. Extreme self-control must be learned by the male through the help, cooperation, communication, and understanding of the female.

Secondly, semen may be released too close to the entrance of the genital tract or the pre-ejaculation fluid which serves as a release and lubricant may contain sperm. It is possible, then, for the woman to get pregnant even though he withdraws before orgasm. This method has the definite disadvantage of placing the total responsibility upon the male and he is not, by his very nature biologically, too dependable. It has the definite advantage of requiring no special appliances or chemical applications and it does control pregnancy in most instances. If the couple can learn to reach the climax in the female and orgasm in the male even when the sexual act is broken by withdrawal, it can be successful. If not, withdrawal can be very frustrating and emotionally disturbing. The failure rate is relatively high and it should not be used if pregnancy prevention is an absolute need for the couple.

There are many mechanical methods that can be used for pregnancy prevention. Most of them have inherent problems of aesthetics, modesty, spontaneity, and comfort which the couple needs to consider before using. All offer relatively high protection from conception if used according to directions. A brief description of each will suffice. A major emphasis will be placed on their proper use and their limitations.

The condom or sheath consists of a tubular covering of thin rubber or latex worn over the penis of the male during intercourse. It serves as a receptacle for the semen as it is ejaculated and prevents the sperm from reaching the egg to fertilize it. It is probably one of the most widely used of all contraceptive devices and offers high protection as long as it doesn't leak, tear, or come off before withdrawal. Condoms tend to dull the feelings a bit but most men aren't bothered much by this. A major factor is that the foreplay must stop just before intercourse begins so that the male can place it properly over the penis. The use of the condom is a very individualistic matter and should be used only if it is acceptable to both partners physically, emotionally, and aesthetically.

The diaphragm consists of a cup or dome of thin rubber surrounded by a thin, flexible spring rim to hold it in place. It prevents the sperm from reaching the egg to fertilize it. The woman must be measured and fitted for correct size by a physician and it must be rechecked a few months after marriage and after childbirth. Also the doctor instructs the woman in the technique of insertion which is accomplished either by the finger or a mechanical appliance. A decided advantage is that it can be placed before the love play begins and there is no interruption in the relationship. It is left in place at least six hours after intercourse. It must be used all of the time to be effective and this is the limiting factor. Women feel confident with the diaphragm because its use means that they are in control of pregnancy and they don't have to rely on the control of their mate. Some women find the diaphragm bothersome because of placement difficulties and others because of aesthetic reasons. Some men complain that they are conscious of its placement and find it unpleasant. The use of the diaphragm is also a highly individualistic matter and both partners should be in agreement to its use.

Another mechancial means of contraception is the cervical cap. This device is a small cup of rubber, metal, or plastic fitted by a physician, which is placed over the mouth of the womb to prevent the sperm from entering. Many women leave it in place from the end of one menstrual cycle until the beginning of the next. Some women have difficulty in placing it securely. Any woman using the cap should have regular checks by a physician. It has high reliability if placed securely and it has about the same problems as the diaphragm emotionally and aesthetically.

A final important mechanical device is the intra-uterine device or ring. It consists of a small metal or plastic ring or loop, which is inserted in a minor operation (about five minutes) semipermanently within the cavity of the uterus through the cervical canal. It makes the complex process of the implantation of the fertilized egg almost impossible. The IUD is used very extensively in the under-developed countries of the world because of its low cost and relatively high protection, and because doctors are in short supply. Not all women can use the ring because of irritation or because they expel it from the uterus, sometimes unnoticed. This device differs from the condom, diaphragm, and ring in that it does not necessarily prevent fertilization of the egg but rather its implantation. For those whose religious beliefs hold that human life begins once fertilization has taken place, there may be some moral questions. The ring is also a very individualistic choice.

As we stated earlier, no device is any more predictable than the user. Many women protect themselves from pregnancy by using a combination of a mechanical device plus a spermicide in the form of a jelly or cream. This combination, although aesthetically less desirable, and more bothersome and not always convenient, does protect very well and covers for the failure of the mechanical device or human failure and error.

There are many kinds of douches, creams, jellies, suppositories, vaginal tablets, aerosol sprays, etc. available on a nonprescription basis at most drug stores. Except for the douche, which is very unreliable anyway, the advantage of the above is their simplicity of use, requiring little skill and little barrier to feeling and sensation. However, all are extremely unreliable. They pose some problems in the area of aesthetics and feelings of security, and their availability at the exact time needed, besides giving to the user a false sense of confidence. Couples should not place complete dependence on these methods, and certainly they should not be used without first consulting with the family physician.

A final pregnancy control method which is finding increased use daily is the "pill." This is the most revolutionary development in birth control methods up to this time and about 7,000,000 American women now use contraceptive pills. Other pills more dramatic await another discussion. Presently we are still using the first generation of the pills. New and more revolutionary ones can be expected soon. The present generation of pills are taken orally for a specified number of days each month; some are taken every day of the month with varied dosage and so that the woman does not forget or miss. The pill suppresses ovulation which prevents conception from occurring. *When taken as directed,* they are the most effective contraceptive known. They can be purchased only with a doctor's prescription *and should be taken only under a doctor's direction.* No one should take the pill without a thorough medical examination which includes a family and personal medical history. There are a few specific medical reasons why a particular woman should not take the pill.

Experiments over a long period of time have shown that of the women who have taken the pill, not one who followed the directions precisely became pregnant or suffered debilitating effects caused by the pill. One of the major advantages, besides ease of use, is that in general, by remaining completely free from the fear of pregnancy, more pleasurable, more spontaneous, and more frequent sexual relations occur. This, of course, depends on the individual woman's attitude toward sex itself. Another advantage is that the sterility lasts only as long as the pill is taken. Once the woman stops taking the pill, pregnancy can occur promptly; therefore, the couple can plan their family with a certainty not possible before. Furthermore, the pill completely separates contraception from the sex act itself. The pill meets all of the major considerations the couple needs to make with respect to birth control methods. The pill meets the following criterion: safety, reliability, minimum side effects, price, simplicity, reversibility; and it is completely divorced from sexual intercourse itself.

There are, of course, moral and theological reasons why specific individuals should not take the pill. No method should be used that is not in harmony with one's beliefs or values. Each person and each couple needs to work out their own solution to the question of how to plan their family.

We have discussed very briefly the principal ways married women control pregnancy. All religions approve of pregnancy spacing and the moral scruples revolve almost entirely around the methods used. The control of pregnancy and the spacing of children presents a problem with which every husband and wife must deal. Of course, children are considered a blessing to every happy marriage. Children in our society are an expected and desired consequence of marriage and if couples cannot have children of their own they usually seek to adopt. But few if any couples want or can provide for all the children they could potentially bring into this world. For example, if a woman marries at twenty, which is about the average age of marriage today, and makes no effort to control pregnancy, she can expect to become pregnant about thirteen times and to bear approximately twelve live children. Of course this does not happen for most women. Why not? It does not happen often because no couple can avoid making a decision as to whether or not they will attempt to control pregnancy; they *do make the decision.* The decision may not always be conscious or rational, or very intelligently made, but it is made.

The major issue then is how the decision is made and what method is to be used. Is the decision made unilaterally by one of the spouses, or as a result of the advertisements in the mass media, or because of word-of-mouth conversation with friends, or a pharmacist's suggestions, or for other very subjective and irrational reasons? Or, is the decision made after careful consultation, first with each other, then the family physician, or specialists, and after a careful consideration of moral and spiritual factors?

The question of method relates directly to the question of how the decision is made. There are only two general ways of limiting the number of children who will be born. First, there is pregnancy prevention; secondly, there is the destruction of the fetus after pregnancy has occurred. Few people would deny that the first is the preferrable way to limit the number of children, or to space the births of children. Pregnancy prevention can be accomplished in two general ways. The first way would be through abstinence, to refrain from sexual intercourse; the second way would be by using some method to prevent the fertilization of the egg and conception through the use of the methods described in this chapter, plus the alternative of permanent sterilization. Few people would deny that the first way of pregnancy prevention listed is highly undesirable; therefore, almost all couples must and do choose from the second way. Consequently, the conclusion we must reach is that nearly all couples do use some form of birth control. The primary concept which I would like to emphasize very strongly is that since we do all practice birth control, and that it is a highly individualized decision, the most important considerations involve the choice of the method which is rated highest in reliability, is least objectionable to both the husband and the wife, is easy to use, is easy to remember, is reasonably economical, and permits the maximum mental, emotional, and physical satisfaction, and fulfills their original purpose for using it.

It is time that we become realistic about such an important part of our marital responsibility. An estimated one-third of all U.S. children are products of unplanned pregnancy. There is no excuse for ignorance today. Why do we go on playing games and fooling ourselves when it involves one of the most important, divinely ordained responsibilities of married couples, that of bringing into existence a new life, a new creation? There is a permissible method of birth control available for every couple who wants to plan their family whatever their religious belief may be. It is up to the couple to avail themselves of the facts and through professional help select a method which is morally acceptable, agreeable, and workable; and then to practice the method consistently.

We live in a great time, a time when parents have the wonderful opportunity to make each child a truly wanted child. All couples have the potential of building a rewarding and fulfilling sexual relationship in marriage without the constant nagging fear of an unwanted pregnancy. This fact in turn can help to make our lives healthier, happier, and more fruitful. It can help each parent to be a better parent because it is a voluntary decision rather than a penalty or consequence of the sexual relationship. We live in a time when couples can live together with self-respect, dignity, integrity, joy, pleasure, and responsibility if they intelligently practice the method of birth control they have rationally and mutually chosen.

For Summary and Review

1. How would you evaluate man's responsibility with respect to contraception? Discuss fully so that it totally represents *your* beliefs and feelings.
2. Discuss the statement: "All couples practice some form of birth control."
3. What would you consider to be the important, positive characteristics of the use of contraceptives by a couple? Do you consider some of the consequences negative? If so, what are they?
4. Choose one form of contraception, the one you, at this time at least, plan to use. Discuss its strong points and weak points as they relate to you personally. Include your reasons for using, your objectives, and the anticipated results.
5. What criterion should be applied in the selection of a specific method of contraception?
6. What other concepts do you feel should be included in the discussion of this chapter?

Chapter 10

What Is an Adult?

In his development an individual does not pass neatly from one stage to another by leaving the previous stage entirely behind. Moving from the status of a child to the status of an adult in American society is not very well defined. Furthermore, there are several ways of defining adulthood. In one way, adulthood is a social status usually legally defined by using an arbitrary age of a person as the criterion. In still another way, some people use maturity to a certain level of development emotionally and socially as the criterion for adulthood. For purposes of this analysis, the author has chosen the latter as the approach for this chapter, realizing fully that other definitions and approaches may be equally valid for other purposes. We have used the latter because in our society there is a certain idealized standard of behavior found in the folkways and mores for those who hold adult status and it is assumed that there should be a correlation between adulthood and emotional and social maturity. There are many conflicts between what society expects and what the person is capable of achieving when compared to the ideals. With the foregoing definition and limitations, we will ask the vital question: "What is an adult?" We stated in an earlier chapter that an adult is a person who accepts responsibility for his or her acts. This definition fits in a general way either of the two approaches identified in the earlier part of this paragraph, but more specifically and comprehensively the latter.

How many of us qualify as adults according to that definition? How often do we not project blame on someone else for our failures? Husbands continue to blame their wives for their behavior and wives blame their husbands and both blame their children (who often in the end are the innocent victims of their parents' frustration). Even the dog, and sometimes inanimate objects, get blamed for many situations that we as individuals are responsible for in the home. By our definition this is not adult behavior. An adult who is mature accepts responsibility for his acts instead of shifting them to another person or to the present circumstances. An immature adult uses the familiar childhood excuses or projections of: "He did it first! I couldn't get out of it! Something made me do it! You didn't tell me!" Or the response often is simply, "It happened." The mature adult profits from his mistakes and failures, as he looks to the future, while the immature adult continues as he is, blaming others and his past for his mistakes and failures, continually looking for excuses to reinforce his feelings of insecurity and inadequacy. Each partner in marriage needs to develop an understanding of his motivation so that through honest communication with each other they might be able to learn to look at each other and grin and say: "You're projecting, baby!" Then we have achieved the beginning of individual responsibility in marriage.

In marriage, one finds a very significant problem centering around not accepting responsibility; and this problem is one of guilt. When persons are not responding or acting as they know and feel they should, they feel guilty. When one feels guilty, he is upset and not able to function adequately. Far too often, the attempt is to alleviate the guilt through the childhood mechanism of projection by pushing the problem off on some other party. For example, how does this often happen to the woman in the home? The woman in our culture is usually responsible for keeping the house and most women do this adequately much of the time. However, occasionally she fails to do this task adequately or satisfactorily, and at this point she begins to have some problems with guilt. The most significant question is: What does she do about this guilt? Often, instead of saying to herself, "I didn't do a good job of cleaning the house because I didn't want to," she says, "I didn't do a good job of cleaning the house because my husband does not appreciate me. So why should I keep house?"

The man is also often a great projector. Sometimes a man may have problems with drinking to excess. He occasionally goes out and gets drunk. Why did he go out and get drunk, which is an expression of immature behavior? Certainly he did so because he decided and wanted to get drunk. But when he verbalizes, how does it come out? "Oh, you would drink too if you were married to the kind of woman I am married to. It's her fault, she chases me out of the house by her nagging all the time."

All of the projection as illustrated above is, of course, perfectly ridiculous adult behavior and it causes a great deal of guilt in us and results in some very immature, irresponsible, childish behavior. All of us have our responsibilities; we have to be able to live with ourselves; we need to progress in our maturity to the point that we can say: "This is my behavior, perhaps it is good behavior, perhaps it is stupid behavior, but I am responsible for it."

Another characteristic of adult behavior is "self-respect." A very simple definition would include "the ability to look at ourselves and like what we see." Obviously no one is ever completely pleased with himself all of the time and we would caution that, if one is, he really is in trouble. However, this self-respect, or self-love, is a tremendously important thing because it is what keeps us functioning; and only when we love ourselves have we got anything to give to others. One cannot give to others what he does not himself have. To love another is to have concern for his very existence, health, self-control, social concern, vocation, aesthetics, and religious experience, among others. Therefore, this must be clear and real in the person who gives love so that it may be returned.

To a point, if we don't like ourselves, we are selfish people. Selfishness results in constant grabbing or seeking, especially for affection and attention. It often is an attempt to buy or get all kinds of things for ourselves because we feel empty inside and we are trying desperately to fill the void.

Terman's study of 792 couples demonstrates concretely to us that an adequate self-concept, or self-respect is a maturity that enhances the marital relationship.* Happily married women, as a group, are characterized by kindly attitudes toward others and expect such to be returned. Not easily offended and not terribly concerned about the impression they make upon others, they do not consider relationships with others as rivalry situations. They are cooperative and not afraid of subordinate roles. They willingly accept advice; they enjoy being of service to others and bringing pleasure to others. Such women enjoy helping the dependent and the underprivileged. Dependable and reliable in the details of their work and of finances, they tend to be conservative and conforming in religion, morality, and political affairs. They demonstrate a quiet self-assurance and are optimistic about life.

Unhappily married women, however, are characterized by a basic lack of self-respect, self-concept, and security. Usually emotionally tense and moody, they frequently have significant inferiority feelings. They are temperamentally irritable and dominating. These women are inclined to be restive strivers and joiners as they display aggressive tendencies and over-anxiousness. More concerned about "making it" than in being liked as a person, they are often egocentric and not interested in service unless it brings some personal recognition and rewards. They have an inclination to be impatient and dislike the methodical, cautious, painstaking approach to problem solving. They are often more radical in social ethics, religion, and politics.

Happily married men demonstrate even and stable emo-

* See: Henry Bowman, *Marriage for Moderns,* McGraw Hill, 1965, pp. 165-167.

tions. They are cooperative, equalitarian, and benevolent toward the deprived, underprivileged, and inferior person. They are not self-conscious, somewhat extroverted, show initiative, take responsibility, and give close attention to detail in their daily activities. They are methodical, cautious, and conservative.

Unhappily married men are inclined to be moody and somewhat neurotic. Often they have feelings of inferiority and dislike being in the public eye. They are insecure and compensate for this by being domineering. Receiving pleasure from commanding roles over dependents, they often live in a world of day dreams and power fantasies. They are sporadic and very irregular in work habits, dislike detail and rational procedures. They are more inclined to radicalism.

The above traits cannot be generally applied to a specific individual. However, the traits are worth considering carefully as we look for the characteristics of maturity that will contribute to marital happiness. A person who is reasonably sure of who he is, and likes what he is, has a tremendous amount to give to other people. The above traits of happily and unhappily married couples, tend to bear out the following statement. The person who has self-respect doesn't need to spend so much time worrying about himself because he knows who he is and likes what he is.

It is necessary at this point to clear up a false concept many people have which has come out of many misinterpretations of Christianity in our culture. The concept of "self-sacrifice" must not be confused with self-respect. The totally self-giving, sacrificing person, so often placed on a pedestal of honor, cannot exist in the reality of human relationships. Marriage counselors often are confronted by this kind of person. The client usually begins by telling the counselor how wonderful and self-sacrificing she is. In fact, it often sounds like a "litany" of praise. It often goes something like this: "My husband is running around with another woman and I can't understand why. I have been a good wife to him.

Every morning in our fifteen years of marriage I got up and cooked his breakfast and I never complained once. I have never refused him sexually, even when he was drunk, etc." The counselor listening to this self-righteous explanation almost begins to feel that she expects a pat on the head and an assurance that she is a beautiful, self-sacrificing woman. (For love without self-pity or self-sacrifice, see: Matthew 5:3-11, 19:19; Luke 6:20-22; 1 Corinthians 13.)

How real is self-sacrifice in marriage? Often one hears the slogan that "everybody's got to give 100 percent of themselves," and when they do, marriage is going to be beautiful. This concept can be very misleading because it is impossible to give our self-respect or our personal integrity away. What happens in marriage when we attempt to be this all self-sacrificing person who claims that he will do anything for his wife? He will wash the dishes, iron the clothes, give her all of his free time, etc. The major concern here is that an element of self-respect is missing – the "I," the "me." "I" am important too. "I" first have to live with "me" before I can live with anyone else. Therefore, the totally self-sacrificing person is giving up herself or himself and this cannot work. An important principle which not all discover early in marriage is that when one has finished sacrificing all and compromising and no longer will be pushed around, self-respect and mutual respect begin to grow. Isn't there some grain of truth in the statement: "Nobody loves a worm"? Therefore, it is necessary in marriage for each spouse to examine himself constantly to determine whether or not he can really give this way, or does he need to respect himself? The happy and successful married person does make concessions to others, but basically he lives by rational, intelligent compromise, and by doing so, he maintains his own individuality and personal integrity.

Part of self-respect is an honest appraisal of oneself, including some objectivity, so that it will be possible to accept the present and work from one's motivations and convictions toward the future. An example of this could be the habit of being angry. Some people temperamentally are angry persons. This poses many problems in interpersonal relationships because the attitude toward anger in American society is negative. We are taught from our mother's knee to repress anger. But what about anger and many other things we assume are automatically bad? Are they bad, or is our response to them the more serious and dangerous? Many persons wouldn't accomplish anything if they were not angry. Once an individual has come to an understanding of self and self-awareness has been built, then anger can be channeled rather than repressed and it can become a strength to the person.

It is so often tragic that guilt over our little quirks or complexes results in self-condemnation and destructive behavior instead of the potential of putting them to work in a positive, constructive way. Not only is self-awareness important, but also an awareness of the complexes of one's mate. A great deal can be accomplished toward creating a harmonious, mutual relationship by encouraging the desirable complexes and avoiding the things that set off the undesirable response. Complexes are not altered significantly, or removed completely through rational consideration because most of us live more by our emotions than by the rational, intellectual process, but we can learn to live with them more constructively.

Respect for others is also an important characteristic of adult maturity. Possibly we need basically to permit others "to be," to accept others as they are. One of the unique things about mate selection in our society is that we seek a person who complements us. If we have certain traits that we believe are weak or bad, we look for good traits in the other person we are seeking out for marriage. We look for a person who is different from us in specific ways so that he can contribute something to us and we in return can give something to him. The tragedy comes when after marriage we try for the next ten years to change our spouse. It just doesn't make much sense at all because when we try to change people it shows to them that we have little or no respect for them.

Probably one of the greatest things we can do for our spouse is to permit them "to be," to permit each other "to be," and to help each other to develop into the kind of person God has ordained each to become. This requires a good deal of listening, sensitivity, and awareness, rather than domination, or coercion to force the other into a mold or pattern. Just letting each "be" and encouraging each "to be" himself—this is respect. It is the kind of respect Christ had for people. Christ was sometimes disgusted and perhaps disappointed with people and especially with Peter. However, He did not try to force Peter to change, to make him over. Rather, He took Peter's good traits and He developed them and encouraged them and allowed Peter "to be" what he was destined to be (Matthew 17:1-17, 14:36ff., 27:58). Much the same kind of lesson comes from a study of the apostle Paul whose destructive energy was channeled into constructive energy as he met Christ on the Damascus road (Acts 9:3, 17, 19, 22:6, 26:12). This concept is tremendously important in marriage because when we finally begin to accept each other, then we begin to mature.

An additional element in maturity is trust. Most of us lack the ability to trust others and so we need to work diligently on the idea of trust. It does not come easily. Trust, in many respects, can come only after acceptance is complete and the struggle for remodeling has ended and no longer is one's spouse viewed as a competitor, as a threat, or in an exploitative way. Trust really frees both persons "to be" themselves because they no longer need to pretend, to hide behind a facade, or to prove themselves worthy at all times. Trust brings security that does not need continual reassurance. An unfortunate thing has occurred in our society. When we were little children we had trust, but in the course of growing up and learning from adults we became distrustful; after marriage we need to rebuild trust in our homes. It is not an easy task because of the many years of conditioning we have experienced learning not to trust. A small child will leap from a high object into his father's arms with complete trust. The same kind of trust between spouses is possible if we work consciously at creating it in marriage.

Since it is impossible within the scope of this chapter to discuss all of the characteristics of adult maturity in detail, it would be helpful to list briefly for the continued evaluation of the reader some of the additional criteria that would be important. The following list is adapted from Henry Bowman's text, *Marriage for Moderns.* The reader should keep well in mind that no single factor is all-important and that no person will adequately meet the potential because maturity at best is relative. Bowman's listing contains the following concepts for our consideration.

A mature person "develops a reasonably objective point of view toward both himself and things and persons other than himself" and is able to function with the awareness of his limitations. He is able to learn from his own experience as well as from the experiences of others in a progressive manner. He is able to integrate what he knows and attempts to break out of "water-tight" compartments holding inconsistent contents. He is able to see various views of a problem and after careful study seeks a complete, adequate solution. The process of problem solving for the mature person is helped by suggestions from others that are accepted critically, and is an outgrowth of his own personality.

A mature person has worked out an adequate philosophy of life, and has some knowledge of social life, its organization and requirements. He is, therefore, able to take responsibility for his own behavior and welfare as well as the welfare of others. He knows etiquette so that he does not constantly offend others by poor manners, lack of tactfulness or crudeness. He is able to work out intelligent compromises in life without sacrificing principles, his personal integrity, ideals or values. He has a reasonable respect for tradition and authority. If the person is to become fully mature he must learn to compromise between obedience and independence and between conformity and progress and freedom.

A mature person, so far as is possible, is able to discern reality and live within it. He does not attempt to escape from it through day-dreaming, psychosomatic illness, or intoxication and drugs; but rather he accepts the reality of change and expects to adapt to it. The mature person "lives in a world in which past, present, and future are balanced and integrated." Infants live in the moment, many adults like to try to escape the present by either living in the past or in the future. The mature person expects and accepts the inevitables of life such as sickness and death and plans for them. "An individual who struggles against a fate over which he has no control is like a child whose kicks and screams do not prevent his mother from dragging him across the room." The mature person accepts the chronological age at which he finds himself rather than pretending that he is someone he is not. Deception is harmful both to the person and the ones deceived.

A mature person is independent and can fulfill his economic role in life. The person who expects something for nothing, who depends on luck, who thinks the world owes him everything is immature. A mature person is relatively independent of his parents and is free from serious parental fixations. He does not feel slighted easily by others' behavior and has outgrown childhood self-consciousness. He is willing to, and able to, endure the discomfort of the moment, to sacrifice for some future gain instead of immediate satisfaction which will cancel out many future potentials for himself and others.

We could go on and on and identify other facts which could be used and related to maturity. The above list is adequate to emphasize the major concept of the author, i.e., that we need to do some real thinking about how to become mature adults and that we will need to spend the rest of our lives trying to get back to where we were when we were children with complete love and trust. We need to keep trying and looking at our basic adult responsibilities.

For Summary and Review

1. Do you agree with the definition of an adult as "a person who takes responsibility for his or her own acts"? Why? Why not?
2. What is your reaction to the statement "that children are in many ways more adult than adults themselves"? Explain and illustrate.
3. Discuss: "Projection" (blaming others). Give as many examples as you can in which *you* have used projection.
4. Why do we use "projection"? How can we come to grips with this in our own lives?
5. Why is "self-respect" so important in marriage?
6. Analyze the concept of "self-sacrifice." When can it become a very real problem? Explain!
7. What does it mean "to permit the other to be"? Explain!
8. Discuss: "Chances are that you will marry (or you married) the person you need (needed)."
9. Analyze the following statement: "The reason I don't go to church today is because my parents made me go when I was a kid."
10. What concepts in this chapter need to be expanded? In what way?

Chapter 11

The Root of All Evil: Money Matters in Marriage

SOLVING THE PROBLEMS INVOLVING the use of money may soon become the most important adjustment in marriage. Never before has wise planning been more necessary because today almost all of life's needs are purchased.

All of us are increasingly dependent upon money to live. Our survival as individuals and families depends almost entirely upon the earning or at least the receiving of money. If money cannot be earned through work, the welfare institution of a society must provide it for the person or family. Therefore, money is becoming an almost constant preoccupation of almost every adult. Few, if any, daily needs are produced in the home; almost all of life is purchased. The impact of a small change in our economy on the family is almost unimaginable in its consequences. Never before in our society has wise financial planning been more necessary.

Spending money in the family is an area requiring a great deal of compromise and adjustment which brings frequent conflict between the spouses. Studies reveal that it takes longer to achieve adjustment in the area of finances than in any area except sexual adjustment and many couples probably never satisfactorily agree on finances. There is evidence that, because of the sexual revolution and the changes in attitudes toward sex, in the future money may become the most difficult area of adjustment.

The use of money resources in the family as a focal point

of tension is the result of a multiplicity of contributing factors which primarily depend upon the personality of the spouses, the conditioning they received in their parental homes, and the circumstances resulting from the continually changing cycles of the family itself. For some couples, the spending of money draws them closer together; for others it drives them apart, depending upon the way the couple reacts and responds to the differing situations.

Since spending of money is potentially a source of conflict, this chapter will deal with some basic principles the couple would be wise to consider carefully. We will deal with actual and specific means of handling money only as it becomes necessary to illustrate the principles. More important than the actual method that is used by the couple are the means by which they arrive at this method. Almost any method will work if it is agreeable to both partners, but any method can fail if it represents an arbitrary imposition of one partner on the other. Furthermore, all methods will fail if the partners do not exercise both individual and joint responsibility for its success. Whatever method a couple uses, it will of necessity be their own, individually tailored to meet their needs and expectations within the limits of their income.

The first principle is one that has been a dominant theme throughout this book — the principle of *responsibility*. The major point under responsibility is to be careful about going too far into debt. Day after day, the marriage counselor must help married couples come to grips with this problem. Because of low down payment requirements, easy charge accounts, credit cards, and installment buying opportunities, debts are easy to accumulate today. Each couple needs to be fully aware of the fact that all forms of credit are really obligations against future income which is never absolutely certain. Illness, loss of job by one or both persons, does not reduce or eliminate the requirements to pay all bills in full.

Secondly, couples often have multiple charge or credit card accounts and each requires a minimum monthly payment. We have to face up to the bills and the only way to do this is to know exactly what the total monthly payments for credit are at all times. This is not easy for many because it requires careful accounting and record-keeping procedures. Time and time again the marriage counselor hears the statement, "We can't keep up with our bills." When asked how much the couple owes, they often respond, "Well, we really don't know exactly; maybe $1,000, maybe $1500, maybe $2000," wishfully hoping that it might be the smaller amount or less. The beginning of the solution then is to get all the bills listed and on the table, then it will be possible to take care of them in some way. There is no other way of controlling the pocketbook except through some sort of accurate accounting.

Financial responsibility for a couple should include at least a minimal savings account in a bank or a savings and loan association, a credit union, government bonds, or some place where it is readily available in case of felt need or emergency. Since it is difficult for many couples to save voluntarily and regularly, a forced savings plan of some kind might be helpful. Saving for the sake of saving and accumulating large sums of money for its own sake may not be at all what the couple really needs. The major purpose of savings for the young couple is for emergency, as the following illustration helps to clarify.

A certain individual was a professional man working for a nationwide business organization. He had an excellent position which provided him with sufficient income for his family and which they spent totally each month. He had a good credit rating in the community because he always faced up to paying his bills and kept them reasonably current even though he had a great deal of credit about town. He felt that savings were old-fashioned. Why should he save money because now there is social security and medicare for old age, and after all, he could go to the bank anytime and borrow $500 on his personal signature? For this man (and many others) it worked real well until certain things began to happen. The corporation he was working for closed its doors and decided to move its business to another community under a different management and name. This happens often today in our rapidly changing society. Now he was without a job and was faced with a long distance move for himself and his family. In the meantime, he began searching for another job which took him almost a month to find. He needed about $500 to carry him through until the first pay day which would come from his new job. He was required by the company to move to the new community. So he went downtown to all those friendly people who had extended him credit so generously before. The first question they asked was, "Who are you working for?" As soon as they heard that he was temporarily unemployed and had a job waiting in another community, they replied, "We really have enjoyed your business, it was nice knowing you, and perhaps when you move to the new community, we would be glad to help you out." Credit, although important to have, does not replace the need for savings. Almost always credit is related to permanent employment, and many people may find themselves in one or more situations of unemployment, sickness, or temporary disability. Most can remain financially responsible even then if they are diligent in maintaining a minimum savings.

Another aspect of financial responsibility involves the paying of interest for the use of money, or for the privilege of installment buying which makes it possible to enjoy consumption now and payment later. Certainly most young couples today, as they begin marriage and later, need major appliances, automobiles, and a home of their own. These both require and depend on the availability of credit and installment payments. The most interesting fact, however, is that the couple who spends a great deal of time shopping around for the lowest price turns right around and pays a high premium in interest and carrying costs. If one does not understand interest rates, one should not get involved in paying them. Couples should shop for the cheapest interest rates in the same way as they shop for the purchase involved. Never buy any item on time, or borrow money from anyone until you can see in black and white, and in contract form, the premium you will be paying for this privilege. Also, care needs to be exercised in signing any and all agreements. In almost all cases, the merchandise purchased on installment credit remains the property of the store until the final payment is made. A general rule of thumb is always to buy from a reputable firm, preferably in your own community. Whenever the word "monthly" payments is used, the couple should be aware that there are usually some hidden costs such as finance charges, late payment fees, charges for processing the loan, insurance costs, discount rates, etc. Credit is never cheap, but the couple exercising financial responsibility keeps it as inexpensive as possible. Wise and responsible buying and spending can add more real income to a family's resources than large increases in wages and salary if they are not well spent. The local bank, the credit union of your local union or profession, your insurance policy and the local savings and loan association are the least expensive sources of credit. If these sources are not available to the couple, they should consider carefully whether or not the expenditure is absolutely necessary for them at this time.

Closely related to financial responsibility is *honesty* in financial dealings. A person who makes a contract with some businessman must keep in mind that this contract has to be fulfilled. We should never promise more than we can deliver. Sometimes persons have to learn this the hard way when they suddenly discover that their outgo exceeds their income, that there just isn't enough money to meet all obligations. If a person is honest with the businessman and makes a continuing effort to fulfill the contracted obligations, the businessman will usually be cooperative and appreciative. If we establish a basic pattern of honesty and live up to the contracts we have made, there will be few instances of severe difficulty.

The second major principle in handling family finances is

that of *communication,* talking over everything and understanding each other's feelings. It is so very important because each person brings to the marriage certain values about money and its use. Parental and family standards are brought into marriage which are often quite different. The spending habits before marriage may potentially become explosive and dangerous after marriage. Add to these the fact that our society places a great deal of emphasis on money, spending, consuming, and acquiring material goods and use of leisure time activities. Thus a real possibility of friction developing exists in every home.

Besides talking over all expenditures of money, communication involves looking at one's own background to find out why we feel as we do. We need to examine this thoroughly and if we are insecure financially we need to know the source of this feeling. Secondly, we can also help our partner understand where his feelings originated. Thirdly, we all need to recognize our own limitations and the limitations of our partner so that financial responsibility can be shared in the most advantageous and mutually acceptable way. Too often, in many homes, the partner who has a dollar in his pocket and is looking for a place to spend it is the one who wants to, and usually does, handle the money. This isn't practical or realistic because he or she really needs a person who can handle money more carefully. Every family usually has one who can do a fairly good job of budgeting and this probably should be the person who handles the money. We need to recognize this, discuss it, decide what to do about it, and stick with our decision. Every couple needs to work out a system of handling finances adequately. No couple can keep fighting every pay day for the rest of their lives, so the best way to resolve the issue is through complete, honest communication. Work out a system in which both have responsibilities, but each does the things he has the skill to do. Any system that will work for a couple requires the participation of both and must be one which both understand, accept, and can live with.

A third major principle is that *the income of the husband and/or wife is best viewed as joint income and considered jointly.* Far too often in counseling we hear men and women saying that they earned the check, it is their money individually. The man especially often assumes that he alone earned the salary and then he proceeds to dole it out paternally to his wife and children as a favor and often in a begrudging sort of way. Many women today have no money to spend, no checking account to use, and no role in the decisions as to how the resources of the family are to be spent. I would suggest that if the wife does the housekeeping, cares for the children and her husband, helps him to reach his life's goals, etc., she earns the pay check jointly. Therefore, she also has the right to help decide how it will be spent. Furthermore, a wife may through careful planning and spending raise the real purchasing power of every dollar that comes into the household. No financial arrangement can work satisfactorily if it is unilateral and imposed by one on the other. Cooperative planning and the use of money is much more contributory to happy relationships than the censorship of buying patterns by one or both of the spouses. Who is responsible? Both must be or there cannot be full responsibility at all.

There is no concrete, dogmatic answer to the question of who should control the purse strings. There cannot be a set of rules to apply. Women, however, do spend about 80 percent of the pay check on food, clothing, and household expenditures. The trend has been toward the wife handling most of the household finances. In many cases this does reduce a great deal of the tension and criticism in the home if it has been based on mutual confidence built through good communication. The trend has also been toward the use of joint checking accounts. But most clearly indicated in all marriage and family studies is that complete control by the husband is the least desirable. The fundamental thing is mutual acceptance of the financial responsibility in the home.

The fourth major principle is *periodically to review the spending plan* you have developed to determine what changes have taken place in all areas of the family spending practices. Priorities may need to be rearranged because the original purpose of a spending plan may no longer exist because certain things have been accomplished, or other new and desirable needs can be identified. After the reason or the goals have been clarified, the couple needs to list all the sources of income that can be depended upon each month or pay period. Next, all fixed expenses for each pay period need to be calculated. For many homes, the fixed expenses such as taxes, licenses, insurance, medical costs, dues, rent, utilities, newspapers and magazines, installment payments, interest, pledges, tithes, savings, etc., make up the major portion of the spending plan. These are costs which must be paid each month and most of them are invariable costs which the couple can control only slightly.

Once the couple has completed listing all income and calculated the fixed costs, they need to subtract the fixed costs from the amount of income to determine how much money there is remaining for variable expenses. Variable expenses include items like clothing, cosmetics, recreation, home furnishings, equipment, transportation, education, gifts, personal allowances, vacations, etc. Only estimates can be made, but they do not have to be made blindly. Reasonable approximations can be made if the couple evaluates their own past experience. If the couple re-evaluates what they consider essential, if they make use of available studies often published in magazines of how others spend their available resources, budget guidelines, standard budgets, etc., a final decision can be made which is truly their own.

The next step is usually necessary. Adjustments need to be made in the variable expenses so that the expenses do not exceed the income. Some provision will need to be made for unexpected large expenses such as Christmas, education, graduations, and possibly a marriage in the family.

The couple then needs to take a look at their record-keeping system to determine if it is adequate, if responsibility for it has been fulfilled, or whether a different way of management needs to be worked out. The next step is to try the spending plan for a designated period, make the necessary adjustments, and to continue indefinitely to measure the success of the plan in terms of what you hope to accomplish. The specific nature of your plan is not important, but having a plan is almost imperative today.

The last major principle is that *the couple should plan their life style so that their fixed costs plus the variable costs do not exceed the sum of the largest permanent income of one of the partners.* This sum will usually be the income of the male breadwinner because his income is usually the most predictable, although, there would be some instances when this would not be so, depending upon the couple's unique circumstances.

What too often happens today with both of the partners working, is that a style of life is established that is based on the joint income of the couple early in marriage. The couple obligates themselves to fixed costs which exceed the male's income. They contract for too much insurance, too many installment purchases for furniture, appliances, automobiles, charge accounts, etc., so that they exceed the total of the largest predictable, permanent income. They purchase a home with high monthly payments, high taxes, and high insurance. They expand their variable costs, including vacations, clothes, recreation, food, and transportation, based on a double income.

Then comes the blow! The woman becomes pregnant, or one of them loses his job, or the wife decides for some other reason to stop working, or illness or disability strikes. Suddenly, the couple finds that they must live on one income. What can they do to reduce their costs? Most fixed costs are difficult to change except where there is mutual willingness to re-negotiate, or the couple consolidates their debts to reduce their payments. In either case, there is difficulty for the couple. On the one hand the tension and anxiety of the moment brings frustration and unhappiness, on the other hand consolidation is a costly process over a period of time.

Both could have been prevented if the couple had planned carefully and exercised a little foresight.

The problem of dealing with variable costs is not an easy question to resolve either. Once a pattern of life has been established based on maximum consumption, it is difficult to reduce the level. Rationally and objectively, it may not appear to be so difficult, but on the subjective and emotional level other factors play a major role. Psychological factors such as feelings of discouragement, persecution, deprivation, discrimination, fatalism and discontent are often very real feelings. Since our society stresses a concept of progress based on increased consumption and high levels of life style, it is much easier for the couple to begin marriage with less and to gain more than to have much and then have to be content with less. The problem is even more difficult and complex in an inflationary period such as we are experiencing in this decade.

It is difficult for many couples to realize that the best made plans of men sometimes come to little. In an interdependent and unpredictable society such as ours, we are not complete masters of our destiny. Pregnancies do occur in spite of conscious and rational efforts to prevent them. Even today, with all of the sophisticated information about contraception, more than one-third of the babies born to couples using contraceptives were not planned. When one considers the first born child, the number is even larger. Except for the small percentage of jobs and positions which grant tenure and seniority which protects the person, job security is something less than guaranteed. Even tenure and seniority do not absolutely guarantee permanence as businesses and corporations and institutions themselves are not always permanent. An increasing number of roles will change in the future which will eliminate, change, and replace existing ones. This is the reality of living in an urban, industrialized, complex society, and couples will be wise to plan rationally, consciously, and objectively, keeping these things in mind.

Money is great to have and is today an absolute necessity.

The couple's responsibility is to use it in the most constructive and advantageous way for their family. We need to keep finances in their proper place in the home. There are many pressures, very strong ones, to have things, to spend money on things. Last year's luxuries tend to become this year's necessities and all of the things we liked to have last year we must have this year and as a result we make too big a thing of finances because we haven't learned how to deal with the increasing pressure put upon us to spend. Consequently, there is a great pressure to borrow on future income and there is excessive worry over bills in many homes which interferes with all of the other relationships between the couple. Instead of being creative and constructive, the use of money in the homes tears apart, destroys, and produces conflict. Therefore, all couples need to discuss finances carefully and come up with a practical and reasonable solution to the use of money in the home. Finances do not take care of themselves – persons take care of finances. Responsible persons deal with finances responsibly.

For Summary and Review

1. Why does the use of money pose such a difficult problem for the couple in their adjustment?
2. Outline the principles upon which financial responsibility can be based.
3. Discuss the principle of "responsibility" as it relates directly to spending money. Illustrate.
4. Make out your budget. Either make it for your current financial situation, or project yourself into your first year of marriage if you are currently planning for marriage, or the next year, whichever you feel would be the most helpful for you. Be sure to include all the *fixed* and *variable* costs.
5. What concepts do you feel this chapter should have included that would have strengthened it?

Chapter 12

Child Rearing — Freedom With Responsibility

Almost all couples desire children and ideally children are a result of a good marriage, the product of a husband and wife who as an expression of their love willed them into existence. Couples look forward to parenthood with mixed joys and happiness. They soon discover that it takes a great deal of courage to accept the role of a parent in a day such as ours. Part of the confusion experienced today springs from the fact that there is little or no agreement in the mass media especially, nor among experts generally, on how to raise children. Parents get support or advice for almost any method they desire. Some people advocate a strict routine in the home, others still talk about permitting unhampered growth or permissiveness. Considering all the experts with "correct" advice, how does one raise an emotionally healthy child? What is right? What is wrong? Who is right? Probably all of the experts are both right and wrong in certain areas.

Before we look at specific principles of child rearing, we should recognize an important guiding consideration. The right method of raising emotionally healthy children in your home and mine is a method that suits our personalities and our individualities. There is no single method of child rearing that is "the way." Many and various methods are effective with different parents, different children, under different circumstances; therefore, all methods of child rearing need to be individualized. Furthermore, there is no guarantee that a specific method of child rearing will result in a specific quality of personality because other variables over which we as parents have no direct control enter into personality formation.

There are certain broad principles that we suggest are important in considering the parent's role in healthy child rearing practices. The principles are flexible enough so that they may be individualized. If parents follow these principles they still will not be able to do a perfect job because they are real people working with real children. Problems may be good because children, like adults, grow in character through problems that they meet and eventually resolve. The path of parent-child relationships is never perfectly smooth because it is impossible to predict in advance, and therefore to prepare for every circumstance that will arise. Parents will need to "play by ear" as they study, observe, and try out their own method. Most parents should be aware that probably their problem is not at all unique and is shared to some degree by all parents. If this is recognized, parents can be more optimistic about their role relationships instead of being unnecessarily pessimistic. Furthermore, parents needlessly worry that every mistake they make will result in some maladjustment in their child. Evidence suggests that in order for a child to become seriously maladjusted he must be subjected to distorted patterns over a long period of extensive and persistent pressures, and not by isolated parental mistakes. So parents need to "hang in there" and have confidence in their method.

The *first* general principle in child rearing and probably the most important of all is that the children *must* know that father and mother love one another. It is a principle that every psychiatrist, clergyman, and counselor who is familiar with the needs of children recognizes clearly as the most important need of any child. The idea of two people trying to raise a child with little or no mutual love is somewhat ridiculous. To try to teach a child to love when there is no real love between father and mother simply cannot be adequately accomplished. To develop security the child must know that dad and mom love each other. The child becomes a comfortable person when he sees love in the home. He knows that dad and mother are going to be there; he knows when he comes home from school there will be love, pleasure and happiness in his home.

Insecurity has, of course, become a catch-all explanation for many inadequate and frustrated personality traits and behavior patterns. However, a child is not born with feelings of security; rather, he acquires such feelings through his experience. He learns it first from his parents and they must help the child develop it. Why do our kids often get into trouble? Why are our children so upset and disturbed in our homes? Probably, one of the basic reasons is that they do not feel that there is love present in their home. Most children don't worry so much about getting an overt expression of love from their parents as they do about whether or not it is present in the home to the degree they can sense or feel it being radiated.

Persons actually search for this feeling of love which gives them security all of their lives. When a child who is three or four, maybe even younger, sees his father and mother kiss, immediately he wants to try it out. He wants to know if this is for real, you know. So he puts on an act of jealousy which is a search for a kind of security. If the love between parents is real, if it is continually present, if it is felt, and if it is honest, it is difficult for parents to make too many mistakes in child rearing.

Not only does the child need to feel the love between his parents, but he also has a need to love and be loved as a person. He needs to be able to grow or mature from a self-centered response to a concern for the other person. A child best learns to love through being loved. All children need to receive affection from both of their parents. Men have a cultural hang-up in our society that hinders the free expression of their feelings toward their child, especially if the child is a son. The traditional concept of manliness in our society contains a taboo against kissing after the child has grown beyond infancy. Both of the parents need to be alert to the possibility of other ways of expressing affection and that a real sensitivity is required as the child approaches puberty and becomes very conscious of peer group reaction. Special language, behavior, and emotional signals need to be cultivated so that the communication of affection can continually take place between parent and child.

The *second* related principle of which parents often are not conscious is that we teach our children continuously by example. A common example, heard in the counseling office, is a woman trying to teach her children not to swear. She had a not too refined vocabulary herself and she mentioned that: "Them d - - - kids of hers were swearing all the time." This is the kind of talk they constantly heard and they simply learned from the example set by her. Further, how can parents teach children not to drink when they proceed to get "canned" once or more a week? How can parents teach honesty to their children when they overhear their parents talking about how they were able to pad their income tax deductions to keep from paying much income tax; or when father brags about how he was able to use his expense account for personal or family enjoyment? How can parents teach their children religious principles and practices if they themselves are only "Sunday Christians," who only drop their kids off at Sunday school and church and pick them up after the services are over? This kind of learning from example soon becomes a habit pattern that is difficult to overtly change.

Parents teach love by example in the home as well. If father and mother show a lot of love for each other, then the children learn how to love one another. However, if a parent says to a child; "Love is a beautiful, wonderful thing, honey. Love in marriage is great," and then completely rejects the other partner it belies what was said verbally. Children see reality much more quickly than they will believe what they hear.

The *third* principle of child rearing, also closely related to the first two, is that children must know that their parents are in agreement. This does not necessarily mean in everything or at all times, but enough agreement must be present so that the child cannot work one parent against the other, or so that the children cannot be used as a weapon against the other partner in the home.

In the counseling office, one constantly sees childhood schizophrenia. The child is completely mixed up to the point that he withdraws from reality. We almost always see in the background of these children an almost total disagreement in the home between parents. For example: Father says, "You will do thus and so." Mother says: "Dear, you know your father is mean. You don't have to do this." In many cases the disagreement may not be this visible. It can take rather more subtle forms, but is just as destructive and damaging. A child who is faced with a father constantly saying yes and a mother constantly saying no is in a very precarious position. The child has a definite need for love from and for two people in the home and cannot be forced to make a choice between two people, both of whom he loves. Consequently, it becomes important for parents to talk over in an open, honest way their approach to child rearing so that disagreements can be minimized and cooperation and support maximized. Not only can meaningful communication be helpful for the child but it will also reduce the tension level between parents.

The *next* principle may sound to the reader deceptively simple or naive. However, the principle that "Mother knows best, generally," is probably quite valid. There is nothing more amusing than seeing a young father with his first child telling his wife, the new mother, how this child should be raised. It is amusing except for the fact that it is also disastrous because what really does this guy know about raising children? During his growing-up period, he had no idea that children even existed because he was so busy playing football, baseball, basketball, hockey, with guns, bow and arrow, etc. He goes through his high school years and becomes aware that older girls exist but young children are a pain in the neck and he avoids them totally if he can. Then he finds one of the older girls, about his own age, dates and courts her, marries her, and suddenly he knows just exactly how to raise kids. We may have over-simplified and exaggerated the account, but generally there is more fact than fiction contained in it.

If we take a brief look at the girl's background, we can begin to understand why "Mother knows best, generally." Of course, we have all heard that the ability to mother is instinctive and you may call it that if you wish. However, more can be learned by looking at her conditioning. The girl begins learning how to be a mother at a very early age, possibly two, as she starts playing house. This she does of course because dad and mom purchased the appropriate toys and encouraged her to play house. She is close to her mother and is interested in children. As she grows older she spends a period of time going through a babysitting stage, either for dad and mom or for some other family. She studies, reads, builds hope chests, she concentrates on learning about raising children. As a result, her judgment tends to be far superior to the average man's as to how children should be raised. Probably the most significant concept this discussion can offer to the woman is an attitude of confidence in her attempts at child rearing. Since there is such a variety of suggestions she is bombarded with from the mass media, professionals, and well-meaning friends, etc., many totally opposites, the mother needs to develop a confidence in her own ability to raise her children adequately. If the husband is also aware of this dilemma he can be of immeasurable support to her in developing this confidence in herself.

Another important principle is what we will call: "Friends, but never equals in child rearing." There is a real need for both parents and children to recognize respect, and appreciate the difference in status which exists. For example, parents are adults and not children; children are not adults. The statuses are not equal and should not be because each status has unique responsibilities and expectations attenuated to it. Parents and children can respect each other, can be friends, can play together, but they are not on the same level. Parents can easily, without even being aware, create a false sense of togetherness based on equality, rather than the fact that the relationship between parents and children is always a relationship of friendship and not equals. It is essential that we maintain this necessary respect for each status or our child-rearing process will quickly break down.

What can be some of the consequences of failing to recognize the importance of having full respect for each other's status? There is a need for "self-preservation" (which includes the "I" concept) which makes every person different from every other. Each person has his own private world, partly of his own making, which he seeks to preserve and protect and which he alters as part of his experience. If the parents try to be too chummy or buddy-buddy with their children this might become difficult for the child to maintain and could result in considerable tension and conflict. Furthermore, each child needs to develop independence. If interpersonal relationships between parent and child are based too much on equality it might well retard the process of "cutting the apron strings" and bring about the creation of a dependency rather than independence. Parents need not view the day of a child's complete independence with sorrow, but rather as a successful completion of a long process in the development of a mature adult which is their major responsibility as parents. Children are not born for parents to keep; they are born to develop and ultimately leave the home as an independent young adult.

Every child must have a final line in discipline. This is a vague principle in some ways because it is impossible to arbitrarily lay out final lines for every little behavior the child will engage in, although some parents may try. However, it is important that every child have a final line so that he will know exactly what is going to happen if he crosses it. Every child needs discipline, in fact every person needs discipline. Besides being a method of learning it gives all of us a sense of security when the limits are set.

Students of juvenile delinquency and criminology have recognized two important facts which can be helpful to parents as they deal with the question of limits. The first finding includes the normal search of all people for limits to their behavior and the realization that they feel insecure until the limit has been reached. What we often interpret as irritability, rebellion, and mischievousness during adolescence is really only an attempt by youngsters to determine what in reality the limits are. Do parents really mean it? There is a lesson for parents found in this fact. If limits are set and if parents mean them, the child will not have to continue seeking the limits and he can turn his efforts toward more constructive behavior. Conflict and disagreements will not be eliminated, but a certainty and security tempered with understanding is possible.

Secondly, studies indicate that the severity of punishment is not as important as the certainty that punishment will be administered in the control of behavior. This further confirms the importance of "setting the limits" as it provides a framework within which the child may operate; and whatever they have been told would happen to them if they crossed this line or limit must happen if the integrity of both the parent and child is to be preserved.

At this point in our discussion we need to look realistically at what often happens in the family which violates the integrity of the parents and child. So often we see what looks like a final line that has been set. An example would go something like this: "Johnny, if you do that once more, I am going to punish you." So Johnny does it once more. "Johnny, if you do that *once* more, I'm going to tell your daddy when he gets home." This response pattern continues all day long. Why should Johnny quit? Why should he stop? He has figured his mother out and he knows that nothing will happen. He feels very uncomfortable because he doesn't know where to stop. He needs to learn self-discipline but he cannot and will not unless limits are set, known, and enforced.

A related problem in families today centers around the fact that the mother spends most of her time with the children as the father works long hours outside of the home. Since she is with them so much she becomes very intimate with them and as a result much misbehavior on the part of the child is excessively personalized. She may feel that it is a rejection of her as a person, or that she has failed as a mother. She may attempt to minimize the conflict by escaping from the need to discipline the child or punish the child in one of several ways. One common habit of mothers is periodically during the day and in some cases all day long to give verbal tongue lashings for misbehavior. What happens when she does this is that she remains frustrated and soon the words are only heard as background noise by the children.

Another escape is to issue the well-known imperative: "Johnny, just wait till daddy gets home." The child then has all day to plan an attack or rationalization to convince dad that what he did was not so bad, or in some cases when dad is a rather severe disciplinarian, a fear may develop over the uncertainty as to what will happen at the end of the day and dad may well be viewed as a heavy-handed monster.

Nagging may be another escape from setting limits and enforcing them. This is very ineffective because it permits the child to evade consequences, it soon makes him immune to the sounds and it provides the child with one of the most effective weapons for "getting at" or penalizing the parent. Nagging tells the child what annoys the parent and therefore the child has the advantage and child rearing can become very frustrating, tension-ridden, and full of failure.

Our next principle is that both parents must participate in discipline. The neglect of the disciplinary function by the father is a major problem in the home today. Both parents have to take part in discipline if it is to be at all effective. Because of the nature of the urbanized family today with the father absent a great deal of the time while at work, we would suggest for your consideration that one of the principles that works in most homes is the principle of "mothers little" and "fathers big" in the area of discipline. In other words, the little things that take place during the day, these mother handles herself. When something big comes up, then it is father's place to step in. Usually this is the only way that discipline works. It may be helpful at this point to illustrate in a very realistic way how this principle works out in practice.

Suppose that the father in a particular family knows all the answers and does all the disciplining. Once in a while, the little disciplines get out of hand. The children are constantly around and clinging to mother's skirt. She corrects the children so often that after a while she doesn't hear herself correcting them and they don't hear her either. It goes on all day long and eventually in every home the children get so they do not respond to mother anymore. Now this is the place where father has to step into the discipline of the children; this is where he comes in strong to support his wife. He comes in and says: "Now look, kids, this is your mother talking." So father is a very important functionary in the discipline area. His voice and manner is a new voice and a voice of mutual authority.

Keeping the basic principles of child rearing in mind, let's take a moment to consider some additional thoughts on responsibile child rearing. Have you ever considered the fact that according to a definition of maturity kids are born pretty mature in a lot of ways? They know how to give love; and basically youngsters are very honest people. But what happens to them? Is it possible that during their growing-up years we teach this maturity out of them? As a result of this conditioning, the child grows up and goes into adulthood and marriage with all kinds of hang-ups and all kinds of fears and distrust. He is afraid to offer love and is continually waiting for someone else to show love; really he becomes a person who is not mature at all. Furthermore, children sometimes are better decision makers than adults because they go right ahead with things without asking for too much advice. Surely, they do many foolish things, but at least they are not afraid of themselves. This is the kind of confidence adults often lack and cannot find.

What kind of children have been raised in the past several decades? Certainly we have raised some young people with the ability to think and then make responsible decisions. But we have raised a large number of young people who can think a little, but not too hard and when they do make decisions, they make some pretty irresponsible ones. Can we afford this kind of failure today? Most of our young people are going to be living in a free society that will stay free only as long as responsible decisions are made by young people — not only in their own lives but within their church and society. Therefore, parents today have a great responsibility for the future.

When the parents of the present generation of youngsters grew up they had very few choices to make in terms of occupation. Today, the young person probably makes more decisions before he gets out of high school than most parents made in their entire life and somehow this young person has to learn to make responsible decisions.

How have we trained young people to make decisions in the past? The traditional approach, which we will call the "Old European" approach, is a good example because it includes both a "method" and an "attitude" which is still much too prevalent today. The method included an authoritarian approach which meant that when the father spoke, everyone jumped. He ruled the roost. It also meant that "real" discipline was present in the home. When father spoke, not only the kids jumped, but mother jumped too. Everything was apparently beautiful; everything was nice, neat, orderly, and simple. However, there was a tremendous amount of hostility, mostly repressed, that was generated in this kind of home situation. The kids were neat and orderly most of the time, but when they could no longer repress their hostility, they rebelled "real good." Not only this, but all of the time that this beautiful, often admired discipline was going on in the home, no one was making any decisions except father. He made all of the decisions. He said: "Mother, you do this; Johnny, you do this." Consequently, the child grew up in this home without ever making an important decision until he was eighteen years old.

If we get practical for a moment and ask a few basic questions we can learn a great deal. What happened to these people when they got out of the home? Were they prepared to live as responsible people? All of a sudden, at age eighteen, the kid comes out of this home and he is totally lost. In all his life he has not made one responsible decision on his own. How does one begin to think things through, to make decisions without experience and training? The old traditional authoritarian home may have worked to a degree in the past, but today our young people have to be able to think; they have to be able to choose and choose responsibly.

To accomplish this we somehow need to combine two things in child rearing. First of all, the child needs to experience more and more freedom as he grows up; more freedom to make responsible choices. Secondly, we always need to emphasize the word responsible because it is very important. How does one permit a child to be free and at the same time teach him responsibility? The answer is not easy and cannot be arbitrarily given; we all need to work consciously at this need. It's hard to permit a child to be free. It's so much easier to do things for children, to protect them, to do their thinking for them, because then they usually don't get into so much trouble and don't embarrass their parents so often.

But how do you permit them to be free? The following example in the first person will be illustrative of how it might be accomplished. Certainly it represents a continuous effort with no success guaranteed. The effort is to help young people think through their decisions rather than telling them what to do.

Now this may sound peculiar, so let me give you a little example of one of our girls, Mary. This is one example I think that I'll remember to my dying day because my wife has always been tougher and better on this freedom with responsibility than I've been. But on this particular day Mary was starting kindergarten. And over the past couple years Jeanette had talked to her many times about how to dress. She talked to her about things that are very mysterious to me because I'm partially color-blind and have no artistic sense at all. Things like don't mix checks with stripes, whatever that is, and things like blues and greens don't go together, you know. So on this particular day Mary called down the steps and she says, "Mommy, what will I wear to school today?" All excited you know, first day, boy I gotta make a big impression on the kids. So Jeanette told her, "Honey, you're starting kindergarten now and we've talked about dressing quite a bit. You go ahead and wear what you want to wear today." And Mary was really excited. "Oh, boy, Mommy, you mean I can put on anything I want?" "Yes, you can, honey." She only had about three or four outfits, I suppose, but she went up and she really did a fantastic job. When she came down the steps, even old color-blind me was kind of blinded, you know. She had blues and greens all over the place and checks and stripes and maybe yellow socks, I don't remember, but she looked like a rainbow. And I would have interfered right there. I'd have said, "Now, look, honey, you can wear what you want, but let's not get carried away with this freedom stuff." But my wife didn't, she was tougher than I. She was determined that this child should learn to make free and responsible decisions.

So she kissed her good-by and sent her off to school. Well, Mary came home that afternoon mad, crying, upset, and the first person that she took it out on was her mother. "Mother, why didn't you tell me not to wear this blouse with this skirt? All of the kids were laughing at me all day." Well, my wife had told her and had told her many times, but Mary had not made a free choice. So this time she did make a free choice. And the other kids had made her responsible for this choice.

And so Jeanette told her what she had told her many

times about this and she said, "Why don't we sit down and talk this over again?" And believe me when they sat down, Mary listened, because it had been her choice and her mistake and she had paid the penalty for this mistake and believe me she didn't mix stripes with checks the next time.

Freedom with responsibility. Let's look at Mary again at a little bit older age. She's in high school now, a freshman, and this time she approaches me and I've learned a little bit by watching my wife operate on this thing. So tonight she says to me, "Dad, I'd like to go to the football game. It's Friday night and I'd like to go. Can I go?" And so I say, "Well, I don't know whether you can go, honey. I don't have any idea of what your schedule is." I said, "You know that you have school work to do and you know that you have other commitments with other people. Do you think that you can go to this and still get everything done that you need to do?" And she becomes very thoughtful, she ponders this for a little while. And finally she says, "If I get at my homework right away I can get it done and have everything else done that I have to do around the house in time for the game." So fine, we got this one solved.

And then comes the next question, "What time should I be home, Dad?" And so I come right back with this same kind of thing and it's an honest answer. It's an honest answer because I say to her, "I have no idea, honey, what the kids that you chum with do after the game. What have you got planned?" And so then she goes on and tells me about how they go over to a special restaurant in Escanaba, it's the only one that's open, and she goes on to say that the service there, Dad, is terrible. They just never wait on the kids. They ignore the adults, too, many times in this particular place. So then we get down to the business of this thing and I say, "Well, so you're going to the game and you're going over to this other place and this is going to take a while, now what time can we expect you home?" And then she gets mad, really mad, you know. "Well, I don't know why I need to decide that. All of the other kids don't need to make that kind of a decision. Everybody's parents tell them when they have to be home. Why don't you?"

This is all a very human instinct, you know, somebody else, please accept responsibility for me. And so then we talked to Mary about freedom and about responsibility and about the fact that she's a young adult and about the fact, too, that we won't be making decisions for her very much longer. That soon she has to make them all on her own. But that when she makes this decision, she has freedom, she's part of this choice and she is responsible for sticking to the decision that she makes. So we go over this whole bit with her and she kind of likes that. She thinks about it a little bit, she recognizes, well, I can do a lot of things if I show responsibility, and I like that. And I am a young person and I don't like parents bossing me around. And so she decides to make this decision and she says, "Well, Dad, I'll be home at 12 o'clock."

So then we sit there for a little while and finally she says, "What happens if I don't make it at twelve?" She knows me pretty well by now and I just sort of grin. And she says, "Yeah, I know – grounded." Simply because she's made a choice, a free choice, she's responsible and she knows it and she knows what's going to happen if she doesn't fulfill her responsibilities.

We like this system but it's not easy. We like this system because we don't have to spend all of our time making our choices for our children. And as they get older they seem to make more choices and better choices. And they stay closer to us and maybe this is part of the reason communications are better in the home. We're able to talk things through. But the main reason that we like it is because we think that when Mary and Jim and Pete finally move out on their own, that these young people are going to be able to make the necessary decisions that have to be made.

Probably the only crime that we ever commit against our kids, the only major crime at least, is that we do not think about why we are raising them and the kind of people we really want them to be. If we want people who are just free, then we need to permit them to do anything they want. If we want people who are well disciplined, then the best thing to do is to start disciplining them now. However, if we want people to be free and responsible, who can make responsible decisions, they have to start learning and practicing now.

Another concept we need to face equally and honestly is the meaning of "teen-age rebellion" and to see some of the myth and the reality associated with it. For many thousands of years we have believed that teen-age rebellion was a natural, normal response. If one goes back to the ancient classics, back to ancient Greece and throughout all of history, one finds complaints about the younger generation, that they wouldn't listen, and that there was no communication. Could it be that we are "scapegoating" or "passing the buck" or even trying to escape parental adult responsibility by believing that it is inevitable? Could it possibly be that children rebelled because of the way parents taught and presently teach them? The child, therefore, rebels because he has to rebel. Much of the literature today implicitly or explicitly suggests that one of the ways boys and girls can grow up to be men and women is to quarrel with or be in conflict with dad and mother to establish themselves as persons. It is important that we evaluate this a bit more in detail to see what the major problems really are.

The most important and most frequently asked question coming from both youngsters and parents is the same. Parents ask: "Why can't I talk to my teen-ager?" Youngsters ask: "How do you communicate with parents?" So what do we see here? We see young people who are going through the most critical phase of their lives as they move from boyhood to manhood, from girlhood to womanhood. And during the time they are exploring a host of things such as dating, courtship, other people, sexual relationships, kissing, necking, petting, and many other necessary, inevitable things, as they are seeking hard to find out the right things and wrong things, and at this point in their growth more than any other time in their life, they need the guidance of an adult. Moreover, at this particular point in their lives the adults they want and need the most are their parents whom they love. It is unfortunate that many parents feel that their teen-agers don't care about them. But they do care about their parents tremendously and they want to communicate with them and it's their most important problem in many cases. Why, if this is true, do they turn to other people, especially the young people in their peer groups? Why do they listen to them rather than their own parents? Does this really make any sense? Why do young people stop talking to parents and adults in general?

Could it be that they stop talking to us because they have found out that in so many ways we are phonies? In fact, could it be that parents are the greatest bunch of phonies in the world? Aren't we always pretending that we are better than we really are? Don't we always have some kind of excuse like "we are busy, I have to go to a meeting, I'm too tired, wait till after dishes"? Isn't this a constant thing with most of us? The consequences are quite easy to predict because the children get into the habit of not talking to parents because they feel it is a futile effort. But then in the family a very interesting thing happens. The young person has his first date and it's to the prom and he gets in about 12:30. Who meets him at the door? Mother, of course, and she says: "Oh, son or daughter, I'm glad you are home; come over and sit down and tell me all about your date and the evening. You know that your mother and dad are always interested in what you have to say." Wow! It's almost hysterically comical. How can a person communicate with his parents after years of silence?

What about honesty in parent's communication with youngsters? Do parents always tell the truth? If the child comes home with a bad report card, do you give him the usual parent's lecture about high school, or college, and of course responsibility, and in the process convey how well you did when you were in school, maybe even that you were at the head of the class? Well, was it the truth? And even if it was did you calculate what his response might be? Did you ask yourself whether this was helping or hurting the boy and your relationship with him? Does not honesty have a twofold meaning in that it includes truth, yes, but also refraining from speaking things which can only hurt others?

For another example, we need to look at mother-daughter communication. What is more dishonest usually than a mother talking to her daughter about dating? How many mothers are honest on this subject? For purposes of emphasis, visualize for a moment this scene as a daughter comes home from a very exciting date. She says: "Boy, Mom, I was out with this guy tonight and something happened to me. We were sitting there necking down at the park and I got all turned on." Now here is this mother, this understanding mother, this honest mother, just like most mothers. And she says: "Well, honey, that is understandable, you are a girl. When girls neck for a long time, they get turned on. I had this happen with several guys before I finally married your daddy." How often, really, would this happen in real life that you would see mothers and daughters involved in this kind of honest conversation? The answer would probably be, very seldom. However, if a mother did say this to her daughter she would think and feel that here is a human being with the same feelings who has worked through these feelings and she has experience and she can help me.

But what do mothers do? The first thing of course is that a daughter wouldn't tell her mother that she got turned on, you know, a mother wouldn't want to know because this pattern of dishonesty is so deep. But, even if she did, wouldn't the first reaction of most mothers be to draw up kind of nice and prim and prissy and say; "Well, honey, you have to be careful with those boys. Now stay away from those parking places. I thought he was a nice boy, but if he wanted to park and neck he can't be so much." The last few statements are real lapses in the memory gap that completely ignore the fact that her husband used to drag her down to the beach, to a deserted place, as often as he could and this is where they communicated and talked and learned to find each other.

What we are really discovering from the above examples is that we parents look back at our own experiences, a lot of which were bad, and decide that our children are going to have it different. We don't want our children to be like we were. As a result, we make the mistake of thinking we will give them a good example and it is wonderful if it is real. But there is nothing worse than a good example if it's phony. And there is no reason for being phony because kids love parents enough to accept us as we are if we are willing to do the same with them.

Maybe the reason we often pretend we are better than we are is that we want our kids to respect us. This is not sound reasoning. If one looks around and observes many families where fathers or mothers are complete alcoholics and perhaps worse, still in all these families the kids love their parents, respect their parents and even brag about their parents. As we stated in an earlier chapter, we need to trust love more. It is sufficient for nearly all things. Parenthood is a vocation and every parent needs to think about this carefully and if they keep working on it, they will make fewer mistakes in raising emotionally healthy children.

For Summary and Review

1. Discuss: What is the purpose of children in the family?
2. Discuss: "There is no single method of raising emotionally healthy children." Do you agree or disagree? Explain your reasons.
3. Do you agree that the most important principle in child rearing is "that the child knows that mom and dad love each other"? Why? Why not?
4. Do you agree with the principle that "mother knows best, generally"? Why or why not? Does this mean that mother should assume the major responsibility for discipline? Explain!
5. What is the importance of "setting limits"?
6. How can parents combine "freedom and responsibility" in child rearing?
7. Why is there a problem of generational communication? How can this be improved?

8. The author accuses parents of being phony with their children. Why is this a valid observation? Or is it? Give examples to support your case.
9. Comment on the following statement: "All of us want to create children who are emotionally healthy. We may begin by presenting ourselves to our children as real people."
10. Are there any other concepts you believe should be included in this chapter?

Chapter 13

Sex Education in the Home

SEX EDUCATION IN THE home may be difficult for most parents to accomplish adequately. Almost all parents have questions about sex education in the home but seldom do parents feel confident enough themselves so that they are able to deal with the intimate areas of sex. Practically all parents are affected in some way by traditional mythologies and inhibitions that limit their communication about sexual things. Practically every parent just plain feels uncomfortable and unprepared to work through a sound sex education approach in the home. The purpose of this chapter is not to give the basic facts about sex, but to help the reader develop healthy attitudes, constructive approaches, and a much greater degree of confidence. There are many good sources available on the sexual facts. A bibliography of good sources can be obtained from the Marriage Enrichment Bureau, Escanaba, Michigan, or from clergymen, doctors, teachers, social workers, counselors, Family Service Associations, and others. Facts, however, are not enough. This chapter will use some of the facts as they illustrate the concepts which are the most important in sex education in the home, but the reader will need to consult other sources for a complete discussion about the facts of sex.

Probably the most basic factor of all in sex education in the home is that dad and mom love one another and that the kids are aware that this strong love exists; also, that dad and mom communicate about their own sexuality and attempt to work out the problems that are plaguing them, and that the kids know that these problems are being worked out. Love is basic. Parents who are seeking a sound approach to sex education need to know that, first of all, there is no single approach or method that is always right for all children. Yet the core of any approach or method that is always right for all children is a continued, reassuring love between parents and between parents and children. In a home where love exists and radiates, the young child learns how to give love in return and a mature love develops as he first loves his parents, then playmates, teachers, special friends, and finally that love that leads to marriage and family. But if the child is not loved, it will be all but impossible for him to learn how to give love.

Love must be communicated and it can be in so many ways. Affection must be demonstrated. Companionship, attention, comfort, happy sharing of joy and enthusiasm, all help to communicate love in the home. All youngsters must know they are loved, wanted, and appreciated at home because if they do not have this assurance, some young people become deeply unhappy, some become emotionally disturbed, some become rebellious non-conformists, or some even become mentally ill. Some young people seek almost exclusive acceptance in their peer groups and often engage in a good deal of unhealthy sexual experimentation as they seek to establish a close relationship with some person of the opposite sex, a kind of relationship they never experienced at home.

Many parents feel anxious about their own ability to show affection to their children and to other young persons. There is no real need for concern if the anxiety is sincere. The need for concern arises when it is but a rationalization to escape responsibility and involvement with their children. If affection and love are sincere, the children will quickly recognize it and they will feel the genuine liking and concern and will respond accordingly. A genuine love in the home makes it possible to make the story of the passing of life from one generation to another full of wonder and beauty which helps to create sound attitudes of dignity and self-respect which in turn help to bring good health and happiness in marriage and family life.

A second important concept regarding sex education in the home is that sex education comes through many experiences which begin at birth and continue throughout life. Since sex is more than a physical act or expression, rather a major aspect of one's personality, it is intimately related to the person's emotional and social development as well as the person's physical development. The importance of human sexuality can be fully understood only by relating it to the total adjustment of the person in his home, family, and society. Parental attention needs to be directed to a very important fact which is often overlooked and minimized at most. The fact is that whether adults give sex education or information or withhold it from the child, his experience of life itself begins his sex education at a very early age. We need to rid ourselves of the naive assumption that in the absence of direct instruction, no sex education takes place. The fact that sex education does take place continuously cannot be escaped by any parent. Parents cannot choose whether or not they will give their children sex education; they can only choose whether they will do something negative or positive about it, or whether they will accept or deny their parental responsibility.

Based on the facts above, we can conclude that children can learn a healthy sexuality in the home. If a young child, for example, sees his mother and father holding each other closely and loving each other and thoroughly enjoying and appreciating each other, he does not have to be told that sex is beautiful or that sex is good or that sex is sacred in marriage. He knows it, he feels it, he sees it. He knows that the two people he loves most, love each other and that they enjoy their sexuality, so it has to be good. This is an example of living what we need to teach and the development of an attitude which says that sex is natural, good, healthy, and sacred. The child then has a sound foundation upon which he can build his own sexual identity.

A different attitude would be the result of a different experience. Suppose the experience went something like the following instead of the example in the above paragraph. A mother and her daughter are doing dishes together in the kitchen on a particular evening and the mother begins to tell her daughter about sex. She has just read a good book on the subject and begins to convey to the daughter what she believes are the important things about sex and intercourse. She goes on to say: "It's a beautiful thing, honey. It's created by God in beauty, love, and dignity, etc." The husband and father comes into the kitchen and puts his arms around his wife and pats her lovingly, or squeezes her a little and she gives him a great big dig in the ribs and says: "Get out of here, you dirty old thing, is that all you think about?" And then she turns back to her daughter and says: "Now as I was saying, honey, sex is beautiful."

It takes very little perception to see exactly what the daughter really learned. She learned not so much from what her mother said, but what her mother did, how she reacted toward her father. This is really how children learn the most. They learn by seeing, observing, and absorbing what we as parents do, not just what we say. Probably the most important factor then for parents to become aware of is that daily life is full of natural opportunities for sex education and that they begin at birth and not at adolescence. Teaching by example, of course, can be a misleading, dangerous concept if parents do not supplement it with good honest talks so that meanings become clear to the child because not all examples are seen and if they are seen, not always are they understood correctly by the child.

As an adult who has a vested interest in sex education, one may enter the task with a great deal more confidence if one first takes inventory of one's assets. Everyone has a great deal of experience accumulated during his own sexual development through childhood and adolescence. Some of the memories, of course, were and are painful, some surely are pleasant ones; however, both can help develop understanding and empathy for the child in your family. The big "if" involved is important. "If" one is willing to remember and face the reality that needs and problems of sexual adjustment do not differ much between generations. It will also be helpful to become fully aware of our own feelings about sex and to try objectively to understand why we feel the way we do. It might be helpful for you to read again the earlier chapters on sex adjustment in marriage, understanding and maturity, as you take a good look at yourself and seek to develop self-understanding. It would also be helpful to become involved in a church, school, or community seminar or study group because a bit more freedom in discussion makes a big difference in one's life as there begins to develop an awareness of the commonality of conditioning, needs, and problems. If there are no functioning groups in your community, you might well take the initiative to establish one.

Before going into some specific areas of sex education, it is important to clear up a myth about sex education. The belief of many is that if one gives a child information he will use it indiscriminately. Of course, we need to recognize that sex education will not prevent a child from experimenting, from exercising a natural curiosity, or even prevent a girl from getting pregnant. There is an increasing amount of evidence, however, demonstrating that good, sound sex education in the home, church, and school reduces the need for much of the random, indiscriminate experimentation engaged in by many young people and does reduce premarital pregnancies. When two young people are parked in a car at the end of the road and if they are in love, it always is a potentially dangerous situation whether they had sex education or not. However, those who have had sex education have a much better chance of knowing what they are doing and if they do make a mistake they are in a much better position of working it out and of going on from that point in developing a mature, healthy sexuality. Ignorance because of its very nature is always more dangerous and destructive than knowledge. Ignorance perpetuates mistakes; knowledge helps to prevent and to overcome mistakes. Curiosity about sex is naturally very strong, but probably more young people get into trouble by trying to find out all of their unknowns through experimentation than they do by having knowledge provided by loving parents and other concerned adults. Furthermore, the premeditated silence about sex among adults only serves to perpetuate a mistaken traditional concept that sex is somehow evil, unnatural, secretive, and is only to be found after marriage. The facts about the reality, meaning, potential, and importance of human sexuality belie this belief.

How can parents improve on sex education in the home? It will be constructive at this point to take a look at some of the common weaknesses that can often be identified in sex education in the home so that strengths can be built in. One of the common weaknesses is that sex education received by children in the home is heavily geared toward reproduction and/or moral instruction but little is communicated on the use of sex in human relationships or its meaning in interpersonal associations, or attitude formation. This is probably true because the facts of reproduction and the information on anatomy are more impersonal and precise. Often, the security of the parents is threatened when the discussions begin involving dating behavior, sexual behavior, and moral and ethical codes. But even at this point, it is much easier for the parent to be dogmatic, arbitrary, and authoritarian in the impositions of "thou shalt nots," rather than carefully considering deep-seated issues and feelings with which the youngster is wrestling at this stage in life.

Imposing sex education on the child is another weakness often found in the home. This approach may be the easiest and provide the most security for the adult, but it teaches the child that a free exchange and interplay of ideas that cross the generational lines is impossible. Education at its best contains free and open communication when the questions arise and are at the moment relevant and urgent.

A further related weakness found in sex education in the home is the belief that sex education involves the "telling" process. There is widespread acceptance of this view. A good example of this approach would be a parent giving the child a book to read, a record to listen to, or a short lecture on sex with no feedback or discussion. Too often the "telling" technique only involves the issues parents are "hung-up" on rather than dealing with the questions children are most interested in and concerned about.

Another weakness limiting the strength of sex education in the home, is that sex education is regarded mainly as an insurance policy against "moral disaster." In fact, if parents could anticipate that their child would live a trouble-free life without sex education they wouldn't be interested in it at all. The fact that sex education might serve to bring about a richer, fuller, more successful interpersonal man-wife relationship, and consequently more complete self-fulfillment as persons, is not often the motivation behind sex education in the home.

A final weakness in our discussion is the belief that sex education is a personal, individualistic, private matter. Those who hold to this view are usually afraid that talk about sex in groups or in the family will stimulate the "overwhelming sexual impulse" and they are, therefore, interested in limiting the discussion of sex to as narrow a scope and approach as possible. Evidence is clear that there exists much value in and need for many different approaches, on many different occasions, with a great deal of benefit to be gained from person-to-person, peer group, mixed group, sex-segregated group, and cross-generational group discussions and interchange.

What then are some objectives of sex education in the home? The following positive and functional goals will be beneficial for self-evaluation and helpful for implementation of sex education in the home that really works.

1. To provide for the individual an adequate knowledge of his own physical, mental, and emotional processes as related to sex.
2. To eliminate fears and anxieties relative to individual sexual development and adjustments.
3. To develop objective and understanding attitudes toward sex in all of its various manifestations – in the individual and in others.
4. To give the individual insight concerning his relationships to members of both sexes and to help him understand his obligations and responsibilities to others.
5. To provide an appreciation of the positive satisfaction that wholesome human relations can bring in both individual and family living.
6. To build an understanding of the need for the moral values that are essential to provide rational bases for making decisions.
7. To provide enough knowledge about the misuses and aberrations of sex to enable the individual to protect himself against exploitations and against injury to his physical and mental health.
8. To provide an incentive to work for a society in which such evils as prostitution and illegitimacy, archaic sex laws, irrational fears of sex and sexual exploitation are non-existent.
9. To provide the understanding and conditioning that will enable each individual to utilize his sexuality effectively and creatively in his several roles, e.g., as spouse, parent, community member, and citizen. (Siecus Study Guide, No. 1)

This is a big order. It can be adequately accomplished in the home through example and teaching by encouraging free and open communication. Since sex education is a function of the total personality, it must be broadly conceived and concerned with the biological, psychological, spiritual, and social factors involved in personality and interpersonal relationships both ideally and actually.

There is no such thing as an ideal sex education program

for the family, church, community or school. Every family is unique, each person is unique, each community is unique. However, careful introspection should indicate areas where help is needed for each, where strengths and assets that already exist can be strengthened and weaknesses eliminated by working them out.

Since sex education in the home is more of an attitude than method, what changes in the attitudes of parents would be helpful? Probably one of the most important attitude changes needed is for adults to accept as a fact that young people are sexual beings and that they need to integrate sex into their present life and future life in the most constructive and responsible way possible. *Secondly,* any attempt to indoctrinate and control young people with sets of rules, "Thou shalt nots," or parent-made formulas will be doomed to failure. Children need to develop skills, knowledge and attitudes so that, as we discussed in an earlier chapter, they can make wise and rational decisions when mom and dad are not around. And *thirdly,* facts do not deter sexual conduct but if the person has a general feeling of worth and dignity as a person he will likely be able to manage his sexual life satisfactorily without guilt, anxiety, compulsion, or exploitation. As the child matures through self-knowledge and self-understanding, as well as through the knowledge and understanding of others, he will find a decreased need for casual, irresponsible, exploitative, and self-centered experimentation with sex.

Certain specific principles or concepts might be helpful to a parent who is seriously concerned about sex education in the home. The following thoughts are intended to raise issues and not to give concrete answers. To begin with, parents should keep in mind that *young children's sexual behavior is innocent* and that their behavior is an honest searching and curiosity. Let's not make it dirty and evil because of the way we adults think because we have been conditioned to respond in this way.

Secondly: parents need to remember they are talking with

children, so *keep it simple* because children are simple. Children are not interested in detailed discussions of biology or the anatomy of sex. Furthermore, they will learn all of the details they need in science and biology classes when they are ready for them and need them.

Thirdly: the best kind of sex education is that given *through the example of love.* Whether the example is good or bad, sex education does take place. If we as parents demonstrate the beauties of love in the home, we will have no trouble convincing this child that sex is a beautiful thing and that it is fulfilled in the marriage relationship.

Fourth: *don't panic!* Probably a simple illustration can best expand this principle. A perfectly innocent four-year-old girl and a six-year-old boy are outside playing and the six-year-old boy pulls down the panties of the four-year-old girl, maybe even with her willing assistance. As parents know, this probably isn't an uncommon experience. Realistically, what is taking place in this example? Most likely the "clean-minded" child only wanted to know what the difference really is between boys and girls. So he looked, he found out, and everything is fine. Mother can easily prevent this from happening again by saying, "Honey, that's not very nice to take your panties off in front of a boy, we just don't do this in our family." But, instead, what usually happens, maybe not to this extreme but with the same connotations. Mother panics. "What kind of neighborhood do we live in?" She screams, calls the police, and says: "Come quickly, we've got someone trying to attack our little daughter." As a result it becomes a traumatic experience for the girl and the fellow as well. It scared the "daylights" out of both of them. The main thing that sticks in the mind of the girl is that when someone pulled off her panties mother almost went out of her mind; and for the boy what sticks in his mind is that he did something very evil, naughty and forbidden. The example demonstrates in an exaggerated way the beginnings of a sexual fixation in two innocent children because of the panic behavior of adults.

Fifth: experimentation with oneself is normal. In fact, for the child experimentation sometimes becomes very exciting. Parents need to avoid the display of overconcern and obsession with the boy's discovery that he has a penis and the girl's discovery that she has a vagina. It is new; it is interesting; it is part of them. Parents become very upset because of their conditioning with the thought of masturbation and as a result they try to prevent it by issuing severe threats of many kinds. When the boy plays with his penis or the girl with her vagina, a usual response of mother or father is to slap the fingers or verbally chastise the child and they sometimes imply if they do not actually say: "You dirty thing." Of course, this does not prevent masturbation, but rather calls the child's attention to it and this approach can cause some severe abnormal masturbation problems for the person in later life. One thing is certain and that is the reinforcement of an attitude that holds that sex is wrong and bad.

Sixth: we have to learn to talk about sex and to handle sex education in a normal manner. Sex must become a normal part of the child's existence. Instead of treating sex in the normal way, parents often arbitrarily decide what they will tell the child and what they will not tell them; then father takes the son aside. Mother takes the daughter aside. As they do, they isolate the child from the reality that sex is heterosexual and once again they are saying: "Son, this isn't something we can talk over in front of girls," giving sex the "abnormal super-importance treatment."

Seventh: a very important principle is one of *closeness.* Sex education cannot be given in a vacuum. A parent cannot refrain from talking to this child for fifteen years and then suddenly sit down with him and have a good talk about sex. Good communication needs to be maintained all through life with children if we are going to develop good sexual communications when they are most needed. We as parents must listen, and listen with interest to what our children are saying and thinking. Sexual communication in this respect is no different than any other form of communication.

Natural education is the eighth principle. Basically, the most important fact that young children should learn naturally and very early in life is the fact that boys are different from girls. The finest place for the child to learn this is in the bathroom of the home by taking baths together, especially if the parents have several young children of different sexes. A little girl who finds out what a little boy looks like at the age of two will not have this urgent need to find out at the age of sixteen in the back seat of a car. Almost all unmarried mothers have had no knowledge, at least no adequate knowledge about sex. A great part of the driving force that drives them into illicit sex is the lack of knowledge of what is under a boy's pants. False and prudish modesty in front of children makes sex differences a "big deal." Relaxed, discreet modesty does not disturb children because they are not dirty-minded adults, but it does help develop a much healthier attitude toward sex.

Ninth: a good principle to keep in mind about sex education is that *it never begins and never ends; it is continuous* in every home from birth until death. It is not just: tell them about menstruation; tell them about wet dreams; keep them from masturbating; and tell them about intercourse. Our obligations as parents never cease and it is important for parents to keep the door open so that our children at any age will feel free to sit down and discuss their needs openly with us.

Tenth: sex education has an extra dimension when it involves God, the Almighty, the Creator, who bestowed sex with beauty. Really, no one should be more conscious of this than this generation of adults because our sex education was to a large extent connected with sin, shame, gutters, dirty pictures, really with everything in the world but God and beauty. Sex was ordained by God for continuing creation, for near perfect pleasure, for total enjoyment, for our total love. He built into sex, pleasure, such as He built into no other human act, and we should never be ashamed to pass on this knowledge to our children.

We haven't discussed either specific method or content and we are not going to because the method has to be your own and the content is readily available in scores of books. Finally, even though the family is considered to be the most important and have the greatest influence, the church, the school, and other institutions have important individual, collective, and supplementary roles to play in sex education. If successful sex education is going to be provided for our children, all of us will need to cooperate, we will have to get involved to help create the kind of ideals and moral values that make human existence the most fulfilling and complete.

For Summary and Review

1. Analyze the following statement: "Sex is never the problem; it is just the place where all of our problems seem to manifest themselves."
2. Discuss the following statement: "Open and honest communications about sex are a natural outgrowth of open and honest communications about other matters."
3. Reflection is always good. Take some time to reflect on the material in the preceding chapters. What is the relationship between this talk and all of the preceding chapters?
4. Do you personally agree or disagree with the contents of this chapter? State your reasons clearly and adequately. You may be selective; however, consider only the points you feel are major ones.

Chapter 14

Toward a Relevant Morality: What Our Kids Need to Know

TIMES HAVE CHANGED! THINGS are different! We are free people! We can do as we please! We are more mature today! We are old enough! We love each other! Why shouldn't we go ahead and do it?

The above statements are but a few we as teachers, parents, ministers, social workers, and counselors hear today. Are they really valid statements when we apply them to morality? Has the sexual and contraceptive revolution really changed the meaning of sex? In this chapter, I believe that it is very important for us to consider carefully the basic facts about inter-personal relationships, especially as they relate to sexual intimacy.

Before moving directly to the major issues confronting all persons as they relate to others, a number of presuppositions will be stated for your consideration and reflection. A number of questions need to be asked to help us focus our attention on relevant considerations.

I would suggest that the basic arguments against premarital and extra-marital sex are untouched by medical advances or social changes. The same questions which always needed to be asked are still basic. What values make for the growth of creative personality? What kind of homes, what patterns of values do persons need for their fulfillment as persons?

What kind of person is the goal of sex, love, marriage and homemaking? What are the conditions under which sex and love remain creative for persons? The question we usually ask, but which is not really basic is: "Can a person have sexual intercourse outside of marriage without anxiety, guilt, disease, or pregnancy?" Rather, the more relevant question is: "How can sex contribute to the strength, growth, confidence, security, and identity of the person?"

With the current emphasis on individual freedom we are faced with the question of how to define the goals of a person free to choose and free to fulfill himself. It is not enough to say that freedom, or the love of persons, is the highest absolute value. A criterion of values that will keep freedom from becoming emasculated power and love from becoming self-absorption or sentimentality is also demanded. It is important to recognize that we come to know God and His will, in part, as we discover that persons cannot grow unless their beings are nourished in response to and in responsible love; and that one cannot know the full meaning or potential of their love and sexuality without marriage and a home. To be fully human, man needs and requires other human beings. There is no such individual as a "self-made" man. Therefore, no human being can or dares treat other human beings as if they were things to be used or exploited without destroying the very finest possibilities and potentials of human nature in others and in himself.

The New Testament scriptures that deal with the "Christ-like Way" are very perceptive as they deal with the human potential. One of the major themes of Christ's counseling to man can be expressed: "Your present way of life is endangering other possibilities open to you and others. Therefore, turn from your present ways, even from some of the ways your present society reckons as good ways, and take the next step forward to work out the meaning of God's will in human existence." We cannot know what loving calls for apart from some guiding ideal of personality, apart from some vision of what enables a human being to be a complete person (Matthew 5:1-20; Luke 6:20-22; Acts 8:22; Colossians 3:6-10; Isaiah 55:7ff.).

What must we do to be human? Apparently, this is a question as old as man himself. It is unfortunate that in a day when we have the greatest insights into religion, personality, and social relations, we still seem to be lost in a malaise. Since our humanity rests upon a series of learned behaviors which become part of our cultural heritage, and are never inherited, we as humans must attempt to discover it. Because this is true, today we need to begin with a more dynamic view of creation, a view that accepts the fact that man is not a finished product, but that he is still in the making. He must seek to make himself more human. The implication in this view is that man should continue to humanize love, sex, and all inter-personal relationships in his own life and in others. If we can do this, we will no longer deny humanity but will aim for its humanization which means approaching "God-like" dimensions which is man's potential. If we do so, we no longer will look backward and be limited by past traditions, or behaviors, but instead, we will look forward, working for man's completion and fulfillment. Instead of abolishing, or denying, or minimizing human sexuality, we instead will look for its fulfillment in mature mankind, to "the stature of the fulness of Christ." In the New Testament, especially emphasized in Ephesians 4:13, the creation of man and his redemption are mysteriously yet wonderfully and clearly interwoven as are the will of God and the initiative of man (Ephesians 4:1-32, 6:1-6, 6:20-23).

We need to consider an important question: "What is the Christian understanding of sex?" It is *the* most significant question because, whether or not a person claims to be a Christian, the Christian concept of man is the most humanistic of all concepts that man has ever considered, and all the concepts that are good for humanity are highlighted in the Scriptures. Briefly stated, the Christian understanding of humanity and human sexuality contains the following concepts. It is the understanding that God created *man* as male and female that each might complement and fulfill the life of the other in *all* aspects of life. Man was not created equal but to be quite different that each might call the other to a deeper understanding and meaning of life and to be a companion and catalyst to his mate. The purpose of a male is to call forth (help create) his wife to be a woman in the fullest potential sense of her being; to help her to discover all the mysteries, wonders, and possibilities in her existence. The purpose of the female in life and marriage is to complete (help create) the life and needs of her husband and to assist him in the discovery of the deep mysteries and needed potentials and possibilities of manhood (Genesis 2:18-25, 1:26-31, 5:2; Mark 10:2-9; Ephesians 5:21-30; 1 Corinthians 7:3-4; Ephesians 6:4; Colossians 1:17-20).

The "creation" of persons and the fulfillment of masculinity and femininity takes place through a long and continuing process. It begins at conception (if not before) and continues until the death of the person. Natural biological reproduction only determines the physical sexual characteristics of the person. The meanings and fulfillment are learned and experienced as the person relates to other persons and as they relate to him and they are taught directly and subtly in the home, church, and community. The lengthy continuing process for most people culminates in marriage as each finds the person who best complements his life and each brings to the other the greatest depth and joy; the person to whom each can pour out his life and in the process discover life's meanings, mysteries, wonders, and depth; and they become literally "one-flesh," sharing life and experience on the only level of intimacy that makes it possible for each to reach the fullness of life and companionship possible in God's plan for humanity.

"So God created man in his own image, in the image of God he created him; male and female he created them" (Genesis 1:27). In the following chapters of Genesis is the account of the creation of the woman from Adam's rib, God's approval in His statement: "they are good," and "this at last is bone of my bones and flesh of my flesh." They go on to explain that Adam was not the fulfillment of creation. "Woman was created as partner and helper." The Hebrew text states: "I will make him a helper as his opposite." The duality of the sexes expresses with a great deal of preciseness and in a highly symbolic way the great dependence of one sex on the other, even in the biological realm. The Bible offers, therefore, a unitary view of man, but within this unity there is a polarity and this is what constitutes man, both male and female created in His image. Neither is complete without the other; together, in their love and concern for each other they make humanity.

One of the most clearly expressed visual understandings that I know about of the mystery of humanity was portrayed by the great painter, Michelangelo, in his painting of the creation in the Sistine Chapel. He painted God beckoning Adam into existence with the forefinger of his right hand; at the same time He held Eve in His left arm ready to give her to Adam who by himself was incomplete. God created male and female for the specific purpose of creating "God-like" humanity through the continued creation of each other "to the stature of the fulness of Christ." All behavior which reduces this potential of humanity is, therefore, limiting and destructive for all human beings.

The phrase, "one-flesh" is an all-important phrase in the understanding of human sexuality. We find it again and again in the Scriptures from Genesis to the words of Jesus, to the words of Paul. It is a phrase that conveys the human potential in the sexual union and in continuing creation. It reminds us that all human relationships, and especially sexual unions, can never be casual because they involve the total person: body, mind, and soul in the most mysterious searching of personal experiences a man and woman can have. This is the way God has given man and woman to share the deepest things in their lives with another person.

Everything we have learned from modern psychology has strengthened this ancient biblical concept. A sexual relationship can never be treated, therefore, as an individual act, for it always implicates and involves someone else in such a way that the participants can never again be as they were before coming together. Once done, it cannot be undone. Its effect, though possibly imperceptible at the moment, is indelible, and continued relationships only serve to deepen its mark made upon the personality of the persons involved, either for good or for bad. That is why it can be said with certainty that through sexual intercourse man and woman become "one-flesh." They become deeply and unavoidably involved with one another in a relationship which expresses their total attitude toward each other and other persons. It may be either a self-giving love or selfish exploitation. No matter how much we may rationalize, it is not, it cannot be, a simple physical, mechanistic, biological, hedonistic, pleasure-seeking act. It is one of life's most vital and important channels of communication and it does involve the persons to the very depths of their personality so that neither can ever be as though they had never come together.

Because of the above mentioned meanings, the Bible speaks of man as coming "to know" his wife through sexual intercourse. In this union persons communicate the deepest meanings of love and concern for each other in ways that verbal speech can never fully convey. In giving ourselves to each other we come to know the meaning of our masculinity or femininity and we discover the secrets of manhood and womanhood. We need to see sex as an expression of mature and responsible love as well as a means provided for the creation of new life. It is through the sexual union of two lives in marriage that their lives are continually renewed and deepened and love, forgiveness, and responsibility are continually expressed as creation continues.

Because sexual intercourse is such an important channel of communication leading to continued creation, it is essential that young people seeking a life's partner and preparing for marriage realistically prepare for it. A bumbling, clumsy, misinformed, selfish approach to sex is not good enough. It is not good enough because it is less than the potential, it causes lasting harm and destroys one of the most important channels of expression between husband and wife.

Decisions about sex, we often hear, are somehow unique and different. However, they have much in common with all other important decisions we have to make. All important decisions make at least three demands upon us. We need to understand the facts; we need to be clear about who we are, our identity and calling; we need somehow to find the courage to live up to our personal commitments. The balance of the chapter will deal with sexual decision-making within the framework of what has thus far been presented in this chapter.

One of the most important factors most of us need to recover is a sense of personal responsibility for our behavior. It is time for all of us to give up the almost perpetual alibi of our environment that we use to escape responsibility. The alibi suggests that we are being hypocritical when we tell young people to practice self-control when they are bombarded with all kinds of solicitations to license by the mass media's commercialized sex. The reality is that they are equally surrounded by solicitations to license in eating, drinking, smoking, consumption of many other things, etc. Furthermore, is it at all realistic to say that alcohol, smoking, drugs, and foods must be put under strict controls; but sex is something to which rules and curbs should not be applied? That sex is something one may help himself to whenever and wherever he pleases? One way or the other, we often try to use the environment as an alibi and if we are honest, we will discover that it really is an attempt to evade adult responsibility.

Some have also suggested that the "pill" has replaced much of the former personal responsibility because now one can be sure of pregnancy prevention. This may sound plausible. However, every doctor and counselor knows that while there may be infallible contraceptive techniques, there just is no such thing as an infallible person. Consequently, the contraception revolution has not really changed the basic issues at all. Personal responsibility for self and others is still the major focal point. Either the person controls his sexual impulses and drives, or they will control the person. Sex may control the person by forcing him into premature parenthood and/or marriage, or a job to support a family before he really wants to or is ready for such responsibility. Sex may control the person more subtly by blurring or distorting his judgment of members of the opposite sex so that rather than helping to build relationships that are most deeply desired and needed, they are closed out, denied, and often destroyed. Sex may also control the person so that the search for temporary pleasure and the ecstasy of the sensual being becomes a cover for a real need and hunger of the mind and spirit. It's up to you, either you learn to control (not just repress) sex or it controls your behavior, one way or the other.

Sex feelings can fool a person more quickly and more easily than any other of the human feelings. One of the most illusionary feelings is that sex is only physical. This occurs because sexual attraction is physical. Kissing, caressing, and bodily exploration seem to be something that can be turned on and off, initiated and stopped, at the will of the participants. The reality, however, is that even on such a casual plane, sexual relations are not at all that simple or just physical.

The fellow or the girl who casually enters into sexual relationships radically changes the meanings of sex. In addition to the tensions involved in sweating out each month, pill and all, and the fear of being discovered, there is the stubborn fact that rather than the relationship being an expression of mature love, concern, and responsibility for self and the other person, sex only becomes a means of possessive, selfish, exploitative, romanticized love and a way to simply seek pleasure without the acceptance of total responsibility. Of course, it serves temporarily to relieve physical sexual tensions and obviously it brings a momentary end to loneliness, inferiority, or rejection, but it most often leads to a greater sense of frustration and inner tension because it is incomplete. A person basically needs to be accepted and loved for himself. Too often we seek this acceptance so intensely that we are willing to give ourselves to someone else because we want to believe that they really do love us. But after a time, and certainly if this relationship centers exclusively around sexual relationships, we are uncertain whether we are loved for who we are, or are loved for what one gets from the other. In frustration and anxiety we often give more which further increases the anxiety. The more one seeks and gives, the unhappier and more anxious one becomes. To be wanted is a basic human need and the sexual drive attracts men to women and women to men and often gives the first clue that one is accepted and is an acceptable person, but the sex drive, when used for exploitation, or when it is exploited, can result in the destruction of this hope.

We are sexual creatures, but this is not all that we are. We are total persons, each with a life to live. We are invested with dignity by our Creator. We dare not be used as a thing or use others as a thing. Human beings cannot be turned into vending machines set up for a refreshment or a lift. To treat each other for amusement or pleasure only is to be caught in the web of the immaturity of self-absorption and ultimately each will reap the reward of lonely isolation. Sexuality *decreases* in the contribution it makes to a given life to the extent that it is isolated from other needs, desires, and values; it *increases* in value to the extent that it does become a way of expressing other needs as well and draws persons closer together as persons.

If the couple finds that after exploring the very depths of intimacy in their relationship they are not suited for each other and marriage, it is usually difficult just to forget. For many, the consequences, such as forced marriage, close off many of their life goals and opportunities; there is a limitation on social activities and growth at a time when such activity and growth is tremendously important for social and personal growth and maturity.

Often the immediate responsibility of parenthood and child rearing (when the child is born "prematurely" six months later weighing about nine pounds and eight ounces) results in some feeling created, others feeling trapped. To many girls, there is always the possibility of the terrible discovery, after she is pregnant, that the fellow she loves, and thought loved her, is no longer really interested. This may be true even though he ultimately does marry her because of both internal and external pressures. Suddenly, sex becomes a terrible, life-shattering thing, quite different from the channel of mature and responsible love and concern and continuing creation God ordained it to be – and it might have been had the couple exercised mature responsibility for each other.

The most unfortunate of all are the ones for whom sex no longer has any special meaning, who can casually and/or commercially enter into sexual relationships with almost anyone before or after marriage and who never do know the depth and power God ordained sex to bring to the lives of married men and women; instead, they continue to see others as objects to be used, or sexual beings to be conquered, and in the end destroy themselves and their loved ones as effectively as a drug addict without ever having their own hunger fulfilled. This is why the Christian faith asks young people and adults to think twice about the meaning of sex in life; just because the majority of the people in Kinsey's study settled for something less, doesn't make this the right path to travel.

Sexual intercourse is symbolic of the commitment of a man and woman to each other. This commitment says: "We belong together, we are one, we love each other, we are concerned about each other, we assume responsibility for the welfare of each other." If their action does not say this, they in reality seal themselves to a bond they are not ready or willing to fulfill. Furthermore, sexual relationships involve a unique knowledge about another person and about ourselves which is not communicated in any other way. Most important, it involves a personal knowledge about the loneliness, doubts, fears, and incompleteness that we all feel, about the love and acceptance we all so desperately seek. These are personal things which cannot be taken from us, but which must be offered and revealed by us or to us. When we wrest secrets from a child, we deny to him a part of his personhood; we need to respect the rights of another person whether he be a child or an adult. In sexual relationships we share the secrets of who we are, personal knowledge which binds us to the other in an irrevocable way. Consequently, to disclose such deep personal truth and knowledge glibly or indiscriminately cheapens and belittles the revealer as well as the one who receives it. For to "know" another, the Old Testament term for intercourse, in the most intimate way is to know as we know no other human being; and since we know ourselves only in relation to other persons, it becomes a way of discovering and understanding who we are.

If sexual relationships then involve the total being of both persons, sex cannot be a commodity to be bought and sold on the newstand, or an isolated drive to be frustrated or satisfied and then forgotten; or, further, an off-color joke to be blushed at and snickered about. Rather, sex is a means of saying something very deep and profound about who we are in a way that both persons are changed. Sherwin Bailey, in *The Mystery of Love and Marriage,* puts it this way: "Sexual intercourse is an act of the whole self which affects the whole self; it is a personal encounter between man and woman in which each does something to the other, for good or bad, which cannot be obliterated. This remains true even when the persons involved are unaware of the character of their actions."

So no matter what the fellows say, after a weekend with the gals "on the make," that this has no consequences, any psychologist knows better. Such an exchange involves the total self, the psyche, the unconscious as well as the physical organs. When a pair kisses, hold hands, or caresses, they are not just encountering physical flesh, but whether they are aware of it or not, they are encountering a whole person with feelings, memories, desires, hopes, dreams, all that go to make up another person. To want another person only for physical pleasure or intellectual stimulation, campus prestige, motherly love or companionship, is to deny that person wholeness. To treat him as something less than God intended him to be, as an object, a thing to be used and discarded, a goal to be conquered, destroys any true significance of a relationship and is a violation of our own integrity as well as the other person's. The current "Playboy" jargon of "making, getting, laying" a girl is an expression of a very destructive "I-It" relationship whch degrades and negates human dignity as created by God. Probably, if there is any sin in sexual behavior, it is the failure, refusal, or incapacity to recognize and treat one's own self and the other as persons.

Closely associated with the illusion that sex is only physical and that the person should be free to do as he pleases is the idea that sex is natural and so one should use it. There is no denying the fact that the sexual drive is a natural, healthy part of one's total physical and emotional being. We need to be aware, however, that this can be a romantic hedonistic illusion used to cover up the real fact that sexual expression is not and cannot be a thing in itself which can be dealt with in the same manner as impulses and decisions to buy something at the store or not to buy. The release of the sex drive involves the total aspect of our personality and any attempt to disregard this fact and to use sex for pleasure only violates the integrity of the personality and can only produce emotional conflict.

To "make out" on a date simply to exercise the "right" of natural expression and for the sensate pleasure it brings leads potentially to a "dead end street." Failure to see each other as "total persons" or "beings" makes the relationship less than human because it is a relationship only of bodies and not of persons. This kind of sex can easily become an idol and the main focus of the couple's relationship together which breaks down or prevents communication and growth in all other areas. Many young couples are heard to say: "Since we began having regular sexual relationships we are finding our communication in other areas is breaking down. When we are together, we don't talk much anymore, we assume that the time will be spent in sex. Somehow, though, we are missing something; we are not relating to each other as persons, just as bodies."

We need to face another romantic illusion squarely. There is a false notion in our society that sexual experience (intercourse) is needed by the couple before marriage so that better adjustment will be possible in marriage. If sex was a behavior in itself like learning how to drive a car, or wiring a house for electricity, it possibly could be true. However, since it is not, but rather is a part of the total personality and character, emotion and intellect, passion and reason, random sexual expression does not permit the couple to respond to each other as persons which healthy sexuality requires.

Even though two people may believe that they are in love with each other, pre-marital sexual relations may, and usually does, result in a change of feeling about each other. Besides the traditional fears of pregnancy, the fear of what others might think, the need for secrecy and often a loss of self-respect, which alters attitudes toward each other, counselors too often hear the comment: "We suddenly discovered that we really didn't love each other." There is little doubt that sexual experimentation, sexual awakening, and learning is functional and positive. However, in far too many instances the couple have really cheated themselves of the potential of what could have been, that is, a happy continuing relationship, a maturing romance, and a happy successful marriage if they had but treated each other as total persons and had not got "hung-up" on the physical sex aspects of their relationship together. This is true because sex following the development of mature love takes on quite a different meaning for the couple.

There are no short cuts to any true relationship that is lasting, creative, and mutually fulfilling in any human interrelationship, sexual or otherwise. Adults and young people need to become aware of the need for confidentiality, empathy, trust, confidence, acceptance, and patience to precede sex or sex may, in fact, lead to the destruction of, and the possibility of, a meaningful, permanent relationship. Furthermore, sex is not and cannot be a solution to any problem because even in marriage itself the problem of sex exists.

We need to ask a very relevant question at this point. How is sex in marriage different from sex outside of the marital relationship? Obviously not all sex in marriage is good either. However, potentially, and for the most part, for married couples it is and should be different. Sex outside of the marital relationship, either pre- or extra-marital, is used more often than in the marital relationship in secondary and hurtful ways. Experimentation, curiosity, physical pleasure and release, manipulation, coercion, punishment and reward, emotional blackmail are but a few of the ways sex is used which certainly is not consistent with building an enduring, meaningful relationship. No permanent relationship can be built on sex, especially exploitative sex, either outside or inside the marital bond. To use sex in this way is not at all consistent with God's plan of continual creation of persons through human sexual relationships.

No one will or can deny that sex outside of marriage has always existed. Historical evidence makes this clear. Neither can anyone say that the first sexual encounters do not have for most persons an intrinsic adventure and excitement that belongs to sex. But let no one be fooled by this. Meaningful sex between persons cannot remain meaningful for any significant length of time outside the marriage union. It is the commitment of two persons to each other in an enduring relationship that gives continuity to the sexual relationship, that gives sex its proper meaning and validity, and turns it into the kind of relationship which develops, matures, deepens, grows, and fulfills the total needs of both. Each says to the other in a continuing way: "I love you as a person; I have chosen you above all others; I will continue to love, protect, honor, and sacrifice for you in a permanent bond as long as we both shall live." There is no time limit to married love. Of necessity, infidelity becomes destructive and damaging to persons because it does not meet the above criteria.

Most of us would like someone to give us a neatly packaged answer to the question: "What do I do about sex until I am married?" The answer, unfortunately, is not entirely that simple or arbitrary. If one would say absolutely and dogmatically that there should be no sex until marriage, a certain percentage of the population would say, and they would be relieved to say: "This is what I believe," and the discussion of the significant issues would end. If one would say that limited pre-marital and extra-marital sexual intercourse were proper, others would say: "This is what we have believed all along" and the consideration of all the pertinent factors would be ended. Nothing would really be gained, but a great deal would be lost. We need to know why we believe as we do. Why is it so difficult for us to see that in essence the decisions we need to make about our sexual lives are little different from those we need to make in all of our inter-personal relationships? Ultimately, the answer lies within each of us because no one else can answer this question fully for us or make our decisions for us.

For the Christian, however, there are very clear guidelines to follow. The Scriptures are unequivocably clear in their denunciation of pre-marital sex (fornication). For the Christian, sexual intercourse is to be saved for marriage and then is to be experienced with his mate only (see Exodus 22:16; Leviticus 19:20; Numbers 25; Deuteronomy 22:21, 23:17; Proverbs 2:16, 5:3, 6:25, 22:14, 23:27, 29:3; Acts 15: 20; 1 Corinthians 5:9, 6:9-10; Ephesians 5:5; Colossians 3:5; 1 Thessalonians 4:3). Therefore, we can see that theologically the answer is clear. Why is it that we have taken so long to recognize the scriptural insights and have not applied them? The sociological and psychological evidence clearly supports and expands on the scriptural knowledge even when contemporary moral ethicists and philosophers seek rational reasons for disregarding it.

The fact that we live in a society with norms and values and in groups where interpersonal relationships based on these norms and values are basic impels us to look at the reality of life which differs only in matters of degree from antiquity.

Sociologically, as we are involved in close interpersonal relationships, modern medical and scientific discoveries notwithstanding, the significant meanings to persons of venereal disease, pre-marital pregnancy, discovery, loss of reputation, destruction or closing out of goals, negative sexual conditioning, destroyed relationships, remain a very real possibility. The writers of the Scriptures were fully aware of the destructive potential of pre-marital sex on the person, on groups, and on society long before scientific sociology evolved.

Psychologically, because of the nature of human existence in a social world, it would indeed be the exception rather than the rule if one's inner self were not affected in some significant way by experiencing pre-marital intercourse. The evidence seems clearly to indicate that today most young people still experience feelings of guilt, frustration, anxiety and resentment which potentially could, and often do, lead to degrees of trauma, frigidity, impotency, and therefore, affect marital adjustment negatively as interpersonal relationships deteriorate.

The violation of theological, sociological, and psychological evidence and insights continues to damage group welfare, results in premature parenthood, in early termination of education, in disturbed lives emotionally and mentally. At this time in history, and in this culture, the evidence makes it clear that too little is being gained and too much is being lost by pre-marital sexual intercourse. Therefore, society must continue to hold firmly to the value of chastity until marriage.

The two basic questions each of us needs to work out in

our lives and answer with validity are: "What values do we set for ourselves?" and "What values do we set on the other person?" As we work out the answers it is helpful to be conscious of the Christian sense of responsibility and commitment for striving to make the best of one's own life; and in so doing, we want to make sure that no person will suffer or be destroyed because of our behavior. The Golden Rule, found so universally in all the world's major religions, reinforces this. "Do unto others as you would have them do unto you." And Christ's command to "Love your neighbor as yourself" implies that *never* should a person seek to harm, diminish, restrict, or exploit another person. Of course, these concepts require thought, study, and reflection. All behavior which does not do this is immature and irrational. God's plan for sex in life is creative in all its dimensions. He ordained that man should live in families and sex in marriage has two basic purposes: the creation of a man-woman relationship which fulfills each, and to create new life (children) to enrich the union and continue human life. All decisions about human relationships, including our sexual decisions, can be considered and made by first recognizing the central purpose of our existence as human creatures. First Corinthians 6:20 expresses clearly: "You are not your own; you were bought with a price. So glorify God with your body." The goal and meaning of our existence, of our presence on earth as humans, is in God and we are to make our lives a witness to Him. If we commit our lives to this divine purpose, we will be free and have the courage "to be," to live out what we believe and know is constructive and beneficial to all men. We then will be able to say: "I am a child of God. I am a person. I am a recipient of dignity and worth from my Creator. I will not be used, nor will I use another as a thing. I will not compromise my principles for momentary pleasure. I long to win the love of another and to give my love to him. But, most of all, I will strive to be worthy of God's love, abundantly and freely given, without prerequisites, in Jesus Christ."

Finally we often hear persons say that what they do sexually is no one else's business but their own. Since we are almost obsessed with the concept of individual freedom today, and stress self-determination in our society, it is not really a surprising belief. But the unmistakable fact is that sex is social because the outcome is always social. There never has been, is not, and can never be a society that does not regulate sex in some way. The regulations may be varied and even polarized, but they are found. The outcomes of sex are biological, economic, civil, political, aesthetic, emotional, and religious. The greatest hoax and deception created by the concept of extreme individualism and freedom is the portrayal of the isolated individual. "No man is an island." Human existence is social. Love itself is social in origin, social in experience, and social in its consequences. Love can never be experienced outside of the social and public transactions in the market place, among friends and relatives, housekeeping, morality, manners, and etiquette, of social life. One but has to look at the complaints of pre-divorce couples to see the intermixture of social factors which greatly affect human love.

In Rostand's *Last Night of Don Juan,* the devil, disguised as a puppet, appears to bring the great lover to his eternal reward. Don Juan begs for additional time. He asks that all of his mistresses be brought back to testify for him, that he was a great lover because he was always in love with them. He eagerly moves from one to the other as they move past wearing masks. He calls their names and each time they respond in laughter and mockery as they take off their masks and prove his error of identification. Don Juan, in all of his notorious love affairs, had never really known a woman as a person. He ceased to be a person himself and never really was in love with anyone but himself. Thereupon, the devil took Don Juan to his reward which was to be a puppet because one who had made himself a puppet to fakery, dishonesty, and sensualism, must forever be a puppet in hell.

The purpose of this chapter basically has been to challenge

the reader to a deeper and fuller understanding of life and the use of sex; to understand the total involvement of his entire personality in every sexual union; to catch a vision of sex as the most complete expression of giving and receiving of human love. Sex apart from marriage is a hazardous undertaking which could have some profound and lasting consequences over which the participants have no control.

Pre- and extra-marital sex often lead to a concept of sex as being only biological, mechanistic, erotic, and possessive. Sex, while it is potentially good and creative can be very selfish and destructive, leading to a feeling of emptiness, loneliness, anxiety, and despair. Each of us needs a new awareness of a concept of sex that is responsible, fulfilling, creative, and a source of continuing joy; and that such a relationship comes only within the shared responsibility of marriage and the family which can call forth in us the highest potential of our humanity. No sexual revolution, pill and all, can alter these facts.

For Summary and Review

1. Do you personally believe that the presuppositions stated and the questions asked in the early pages of this chapter are vital? Why or why not? Explain!
2. What does it mean "to be human"?
3. Evaluate the concept of "continual creation." State clearly and completely your views.
4. Discuss the concept of "one-flesh."
5. How are the decisions we make about sex different from other inter-personal decisions we have to make?
6. Discuss in full the concept of "sexual responsibility."
7. Why is sexual intercourse symbolic of "commitment"?
8. Why cannot sex be only "physical"?
9. What basically do we have to know to make rational decisions about anything?
10. What other concepts do you think should be included in this chapter?

A Bibliography of Recommended Books, Filmstrips and Recordings

Books

Bailey, Derrick Sherwin, *The Mystery of Love and Marriage* (New York: Harper & Row, 1952).

———, *Sexual Relation in Christian Thought* (New York: Harper & Brothers, 1959).

Bertocci, Peter A., *The Human Venture in Sex, Love, and Marriage* (New York: Association Press, 1949).

———, *Sex, Love, and the Person* (New York: Sheed and Ward, 1967).

Bird, Caroline, *Born Female* (New York: David McKay Company, Inc., 1969).

Blood, Robert O., *Husbands and Wives* (New York: Free Press, 1960).

———, *Marriage* (New York: Free Press, second edition, 1969).

Bowman, Henry A., *Marriage for Moderns* (New York: McGraw-Hill Book Company, sixth edition, 1970).

Bueltmann, A. J., *Take the High Road* (St. Louis: Concordia Publishing House, 1967), Concordia Sex Education Series, for junior high.

Calderone, Mary S., *Release From Sexual Tension* (New York: Random House, 1960).

Catoir, Fr. John and Jose de Vinck, *The Challenge of Love* (New York: Hawthorn Books, Inc., 1969).

Cavan, Ruth Shonle, *The American Family* (New York: Thomas Y. Crowell Company, fourth edition, 1969).

———, *Marriage and Family in the Modern World: A Book of Readings* (New York: Thomas Y. Crowell Company, third edition, 1969).

Christensen, Harold T., *Handbook of Marriage and the Family* (Chicago: Rand McNally, 1964).

———, *Marriage Analysis* (New York: Ronald Press, 1958).

Clinebell, Howard J. and Charlotte H., *The Intimate Marriage* (New York: Harper & Row, 1970).

Cole, William Graham, *Sex and Love in the Bible* (New York: Association Press, 1959).

———, *Sex in Christianity and Psychoanalysis* (New York: Oxford University Press, 1966).

Deen, Edith, *Family Living in the Bible* (New York: Harper & Row, 1963).

Demant, V. A., *Christian Sex Ethics* (New York: Harper & Row, 1963).

Deutch, Helene, *The Psychology of Women* (New York: Grune & Stratton, 1944).

Duvall, Evelyn M., *Family Development* (Chicago: Lippincott, third edition, 1967).

———, *Love and the Facts of Life* (New York: Association Press, 1963).

———, *Today's Teen-agers* (New York: Association Press, 1966).

———, *Why Wait Till Marriage* (New York: Association Press, 1965).

Duvall, Evelyn M. and Reuben Hill, *Being Married* (New York: Association Press, 1960).

Duvall, Evelyn M. and Joy Johnson, *The Art of Dating* (New York: Association Press, revised edition, 1967).

Duvall, Sylvanus M., *Before You Marry* (New York: Association Press, 1959).

Eller, Vernard, *The Mad Morality: Or the Ten Commandments Revisited* (Nashville: Abingdon Press, 1970).

Fairchild, Roy W., *Christians in Families* (Richmond: Covenant Life Curriculum, 1964).

Fairchild, Roy W. and John Charles Wynn, *Families in the Church: A Protestant Survey* (New York: Association Press, 1961).

Feucht, Oscar, ed., *Sex and the Church* (St. Louis: Concordia Publishing House, 1961).

Freeman, Lucy, *Emotional Maturity in Love and Marriage* (New York: Harper, 1961).

Frey, Marguerite K., *I Wonder, I Wonder* (St. Louis: Concordia Publishing House, 1967), Concordia Sex Education Series, grades K-3.

Fromm, Erich, *The Art of Loving* (New York: Harper, 1956).

Genné, William and Elizabeth, eds., *Christians and the Crisis in Sex Morality* (New York: Association Press, 1957).

Ginott, Haim G., *Between Parent and Child* (New York: Macmillan, 1965).

Godard, James M., *The Blue Light, Christian Dimensions in Marriage* (Richmond: Covenant Life Curriculum, 1964).

Granberg, Lars I., *For Adults Only* (Grand Rapids: Zondervan Publishing House, 1971).

Guttmacher, Alan F., *Birth Control and Love* (New York: Macmillan, 1969).

Hadden, Jeffrey K. and Marie L. Borgatta, eds., *Marriage and the Family: A Comprehensive Reader* (Itasca, Illinois: F. E. Peacock Publishers, 1969).

Haring, Bernhard, *Toward a Christian Moral Theology* (Notre Dame: University of Notre Dame Press, 1966).

Heiss, Jerold, *Family Roles and Interaction: An Anthology* (Chicago: Rand McNally & Co., 1968).

Hettlinger, Richard F., *Living With Sex: The Students' Dilemma* (New York: Seabury Press, 1966).

Hiltner, Seward, *The Context of Pastoral Counseling* (New York: Abingdon Press, 1961).

———, *Sex and the Christian Life* (New York: Association Press, 1957).

Hummel, Ruth, *Wonderfully Made* (St. Louis: Concordia Publishing House, 1967), Concordia Sex Education Series, grades 4-6.

Johnson, Cecil E., *Sex and Human Relationships* (Columbus, Ohio: Charles E. Merrill Publishing Company, 1970).

Johnson, Dean, *Marriage Counseling: Theory and Practice* (Englewood Cliffs: Prentice Hall, 1961).

Kephart, William M., *The Family, Society, and the Individual* (Boston: Houghton Mifflin Company, second edition, 1966).

Kirkpatrick, Clifford, *The Family: As Process and Institution* (New York: Ronald Press, 1963).

Kolb, Erwin J., *Parent's Guide to Christian Conversation About Sex* (St. Louis: Concordia Publishing House, 1967), Concordia Sex Education Series, book five.

Kronhausen, Eberhard and Phyllis, *The Sexually Responsive Woman* (New York: Grove Press, 1964).

Landis, Judson T. and Mary G., *Building a Successful Marriage* (Englewood Cliffs: Prentice Hall, 1958).

———, *Teen-ager's Guide for Living* (Englewood Cliffs: Prentice Hall, 1957).

Landis, Paul H., *Guide to Making the Most of Marriage* (New York: Appleton Century-Crofts, fourth edition, 1970).

———, *Teen Love—Teen Marriage* (New York: Grossett & Dunlop, 1966).

LeShan, Eda J., *How to Survive Parenthood* (New York: Random House, 1965).

Leslie, Gerald R., *The Family in Social Context* (New York: Oxford University Press, 1967).

Mace, David Robert, *The Christian Response to the Sexual Revolution* (Nashville: Abingdon, 1970).
———, *Marriage: East and West* (Garden City: Doubleday, 1960).
———, *Whom God Hath Joined* (Philadelphia: Westminster Press, 1953).
Maurois, Andre, *The Art of Living* (New York: Harper & Row, 1940).
Miles, Herbert, *Sexual Happiness in Marriage* (Grand Rapids: Zondervan Publishing House, 1967).
Monsma, John C., *Religion and Birth Control* (Garden City: Doubleday, 1963).
Narramore, Clyde M., *How to Tell Your Children About Sex* (Grand Rapids: Zondervan Publishing House, 1958).
Niebuhr, H. Richard, *The Responsible Self* (New York: Harper & Row, 1963).
Peterson, James Alfred, *Education for Marriage* (New York: Scribner, second edition, 1964).
Peterson, James A., ed., *Marriage and Family Counseling: Perspective and Prospect* (New York: Association Press, 1968).
Piper, Otto A., *The Biblical View of Sex and Marriage* (New York: Charles Scribner's Sons, 1960).
Price, Eugenia, *God Speaks to Women Today* (Grand Rapids: Zondervan Publishing House, 1964).
———, *Woman to Woman* (Grand Rapids: Zondervan Publishing House, 1959).
Rainwater, Lee, *Family Design: Marital Sexuality, Family Size, and Contraception* (Chicago: Aldine Publishing Co., 1965).
Reiber, Stanley Robert, *Toward Understanding Sex* (Richmond: Covenant Life Curriculum, 1964), for grades 7-9.
Reiss, Ira L., *The Family System in America* (New York: Holt, Rinehart and Winston, 1971).
———, *Premarital Sexual Standards in America* (New York: Free Press, 1960).
———, *The Social Context of Premarital Permissiveness* (New York: Holt, Rinehart and Winston, 1967).
Robinson, John, *Christian Freedom in a Permissive Society* (Philadelphia: Westminster Press, 1970).
———, *Christian Morals Today* (Philadelphia: Westminster Press, 1964).
———, *Honest to God* (Philadelphia: Westminster Press, 1963).
Rutledge, A. L., *Pre-marital Counseling* (Cambridge: Schenkman Publishing Company, 1966).
Satir, Virginia, *Conjoint Family Therapy* (Palo Alto: Science and Behavior Books, Inc., 1964).

Schwarz, Berthold E. and Bartholomew A. Ruggieri, *You Can Raise Decent Children* (New Rochelle: Arlington House, 1971).

Scudder, C. W., *The Family in Christian Perspective* (Nashville: Broadman Press, 1962).

Shedd, Charlie W., *Letters to Karen: On Keeping Love in Marriage* (New York: Abingdon Press, 1970).

———, *Letters to Phillip: On How to Treat a Woman* (New York: Doubleday & Company, Inc., 1968).

———, *Promises to Peter: Building a Bridge From Parent to Child* (Waco: Word Books, 1970).

Sherrill, Helen Hardwicke, *Christian Parenthood: A Lifetime Guide* (Richmond: Covenant Life Curriculum, 1964).

Steinmetz, Urban G., *"I Will": The Present and Future of Marriage* (Notre Dame: Ave Maria Press, 1969).

———, *Let's Talk About Sex: A Discussion Program for Parents and Teachers* (Notre Dame: Fides Publishers, Inc., 1968).

———, *The Male Mystique* (Notre Dame: Ave Maria Press and Twenty-Third Publications, 1970).

———, *With Marriage in Mind: A Discussion Program* (Notre Dame: Fides Publishers, Inc., 1968).

Stewart, Charles William, *The Minister as Marriage Counselor* (Nashville: Abingdon, 1970).

Tenenbaum, Samuel, *A Psychologist Looks at Marriage* (New York: A. S. Barnes and Company, 1968).

Thielicke, Helmut, *The Ethics of Sex* (New York: Harper & Row, 1964).

Tooman, Charles L., *That Plot of Ground: Moral Dilemmas for Married People* (St. Meinrad, Indiana: Abbey Press, 1970).

Udry, J. Richard, *The Social Context of Marriage* (Philadelphia and New York: J. B. Lippincott Company, 1966).

Vincent, Clark E., *Unmarried Mothers* (New York: Free Press, 1961).

Vincent, M. V., *God, Sex and You* (Philadelphia: J. B. Lippincott Company, 1971).

Weisser, Eric, *Pregnancy: Conception and Heredity* (New York: Blaisdell Publishing Company, 1965).

Wessler, Martin F., *Christian View of Sex Education* (St. Louis: Concordia Publishing House, 1968), Concordia Sex Education Series, book six.

Williamson, Robert C., *Marriage and Family Relations* (New York: John Wiley & Sons, Inc., 1966).

Wills, Ann McCelvey, *Dear Superniki Purple: Answers to Personal Questions* (Wheaton: Tyndale House Publishers, 1971).

Winch, Robert F., *The Modern Family* (New York: Holt, Rinehart and Winston, Inc., third edition, 1971).

Winch, Robert and Louis Wolf Goodman, *Selected Studies in Marriage and the Family* (New York: Holt, Rinehart and Winston, Inc., 1968).
Winter, Gibson, *Elements for a Social Ethic* (New York: Macmillan, 1966).
———, *Love and Conflict: New Patterns in Family Life* (Garden City: Doubleday, 1958).
Witt, Elmer N., *Life Can Be Sexual* (St. Louis: Concordia Publishing House, 1967), Concordia Sex Education Series, high school.
Womble, Dale L., *Foundations for Marriage and Family Relations* (New York: Macmillan, 1966).
Wood, Leland F., *How Love Grows in Marriage* (New York: Macmillan, 1950).
Zuk, Gerald H., *Family Therapy and Disturbed Families* (Palo Alto: Science and Behavior Books, Inc., 1967).

Filmstrips and Recordings

Concordia Sex Education Series — Correlated sound filmstrips and long play records. Produced by the Concordia Publishing House, St. Louis, Missouri.

1. *I Wonder, I Wonder* (5-8)
2. *Wonderfully Made* (9-11)
3. *Take the High Road* (12-14)
4. *Parent's Guide to Christian Conversation About Sex*

RECORDED PROGRAMS PRODUCED BY THE FAMILY ENRICHMENT BUREAU, ESCANABA, MICHIGAN. Write for a catalogue. Their address is 1615 Ludington Street, 49829. All recordings are approximately twenty minutes in length.

Adult Enrichment Seminar, Volume I, *The Family*

1. The Church and the Home
2. The Adult Enrichment Seminar
3. Marriage Is Real
4. A Formula for Building Love in the Home
5. Thinking About Talking
6. Improving Communication
7. A Complicated Me
8. The Many Meanings of Sexual Intercourse
9. Thinking About Sexual Intercourse
10. The Total Climax of Love

11. What Is an Adult?
12. Thoughts on Child-rearing — "Freedom With Responsibility"
13. Creating Emotionally Healthy Children
14. Sex Education in the Home

(As indicated in the *Preface*, a substantial portion of the book is based on the concepts found in the above taped program. The book and the tapes are inseparable tools for successful group discussion and leadership training.)

ADULT ENRICHMENT SEMINAR, VOLUME II, *The Christian as a Person*

1. What Gear Am I In?
2. There's No Escape
3. See What You Made Me Do!
4. Who's Responsible for What I Do?
5. Destroying Communications
6. Building Communications
7. Making Moral Decisions
8. Married Sexuality
9. Getting Involved
10. Being Christian

YOUNG ADULT SEMINAR, VOLUME I, *Thinking About Marriage*

1. Thinking About Marriage
2. Looking at Other Marriages
3. Taking a Look at Me
4. The Married Person's Prayer
5. Becoming a Woman
6. Becoming a Man
7. The Many Meanings of Sexual Intercourse
8. Thinking About the Love Story

(You must have *The Family* in order to use this kit)

TOWARD MARRIAGE

1. The Last Long Mile
2. The Honeymoon Is Real, Too
3. Learning to Talk to Each Other
4. Your Sexual Communications
5. Understanding Ourselves as Sexual People
6. A Lot of Little Things

YOUNG ADULT ENRICHMENT PROGRAM (grades 8-10)

1. Sex Is a Simple Thing
2. The Girl Matures
3. The Boy Matures
4. The Man and Woman Get Married
5. Understanding Ourselves as Sexual People
6. Responsible Sexual Behavior

UNDERSTANDING OUR SEXUALITY (grades 5-8)

1. Learning to Love
2. The Girl Grows Up
3. The Boy Grows Up
4. Becoming a Young Adult

MARRIAGE, ARE YOU SERIOUS?

Five cassettes covering:

1. Dream World Stage
2. Disillusion
3. Misery
4. Awakening
5. The Time of Love

The tapes are an expansion on the concepts the author discusses in Chapter 1, *Marriage Is Real*

THE FAMILY MEETING

Five cassettes covering:

1. Conversations with a teenager
2. Conversations with a father
3. Conversations with a marriage counselor
4. Conversations with a guidance counselor
5. The insights of Urb Steinmetz

Index

acceptance
basic need of, 22, 23
illustration of, 23
adult
and selfishness, 135
and self-respect, 134
definition of, 132
immature behavior of, 133
anger
dealing with, 137, 138
antagonistic cooperation, 63
Apostle Paul
channeling of energy, 139
attitude toward marriage
lifetime of cooperation, 15
will to succeed, 15, 16
avoidance
as a barrier to communication, 55
consequences of, 56
examples of, 55, 56
feigning tiredness as a form of, 57
social activity as a form of, 56
television an instrument of, 57

"bad fight"
avoidance of, 47
example of, 46
Bailey, Sherwin, 197
birth control
coitus interruptus, 124
cervical cap, 126
combinations of, 127
condom, 125
diaphragm, 125, 126
how the decision to use is made, 129
important considerations, 130
individualized decision, 130
intra-uterine device, 126
limiting or spacing, 129
man's role and responsibility, 118
marital responsibility, 130
need for counseling, 119
physical welfare of the mother, 120
pill, 127, 128
plan for all couples, 130
pregnancy prevention, 129
questions on usage, 118, 119
religious considerations, 128, 129
rhythm method, 120-124
reasons for use, 118, 119
sexual adjustment and, 119, 120
Bowman, Henry, 70, 135, 140
building one's partner
positive results, 32

castrated male, 108
change
danger of coercion, 33
fear and willingness to, 13
nonsense of forcing, 34
not immediate, 22
positive attitude toward, 13
through love, 33
why persons change in marriage, 33, 34
child rearing
basic issues, 168
both parents participate, 162, 163
certainty of punishment, 161
child's search for love, 156
current confusion about, 154
dealing with child's insecurity, 156
dealing with responsibility, 166-168
father's role, 162, 163
female conditioning for, 159

final line on discipline, 160, 161
freedom and responsibility, 165-168
"friends but never equals," 159, 160
honesty in, 169-171
independence and maturation, 160
integrity of parents in, 161, 162
kids are mature, 163, 164
knowing mom and dad love one another, 155, 156
male conditioning for, 158, 159
mother knows best, 158
mother's need for confidence in, 159
mother's role and personalization, 162, 163
nagging, 162
need for guidance, 169
need for parents' agreement in, 158
need to be loved and to love, 156, 157
no single method of, 154, 155
parent-child communication in, 169
"playing by ear," 155
pretending in, 172
principles for, 155ff.
problems not unique, 155
setting limits, 161
self-preservation and privacy, 160
teaching by example, 157
teen-age rebellion, 169
today's children, 164
tongue-lashings and threats, 162
traditional approach to, 164
Christian response to God, 37
Christ's respect for others, 139
climax, orgasm, 87
clitoris, 86
coitus interruptus
advantages, 124
disadvantages, 125
need for self-control in, 124
commitment to God, 203
communication
accuracy and volume of, 26, 27
awareness of content, 31
basic parts of, 27
courage to be real in, 42, 43
habit of, 43
hard work and, 31
honesty in, 28
improving, 50, 51
incompleteness of, 39
male conditioning, 44
need for motivation, 31
need to consciously build, 39
need to understand degrees of difference, 35
questions to ask for improvement, 50
sarcasm in, 51
selective, 27
sensitivity and tolerance in, 43
use of "love words," 44
volume not crucial, 27
with God, 36
with love, 44
with our partner, 30, 31
with self, 27, 28
communication problems
assumptions, 35
awareness of partner, 30, 31
condemnation, 35
criticism, 35
defensiveness, 41
hiding behind facades, 30
listening, 40, 41
logic and feelings, 35
principle of "right and wrong," 35
projection, 28, 29, 35
taking each other for granted, 44
compatibility
myth of, 16
reality of, 14
complexes
dealing with, 138
recognition of, 138
complementarity, 34
compulsive talker
characteristics and needs, 58, 59
conditioning
"crazy clean" syndrome, 66
criticism, 67

examples from counseling, 66, 67
facing up to the facts, 70
guilt, 68, 69
individual a product of experience, 62, 63
male attitudes, 67
mother- and father-in-law problem, 68
need for self-understanding, 70
parents' role in, 63ff.
response to, 65, 66
suspicion, 67
understanding origins, 67
condom, 125
conflict resolution
approaches guaranteeing failure, 48, 49
conflict with authority, 33
"conspiracy of silence"
as a barrier to communication, 57
contraception
external considerations, 120
inherent problems, 125
non-prescription variety, 127
sexual revolution and, 119
the decision to use, 119
creative conflict, 45, 46
credit
cheapest sources, 147
facts to consider, 147
cultural conditioning
fighting, 45
negative aspects, 45, 46
positive aspects, 45

deification of "mom," 64
diaphragm, 126
dictating to God in prayer, 37
differences
acceptance of, 14, 15
potentials, 15
resolving of, 21
dishonesty
as a barrier to communication, 54, 55
examples of in communication, 55
exploitative, 55
in communication, 42
divorce
cause of, 19
"dream world stage"
description of, 17
honeymoon myth, 17, 18
"kiss and make up" solutions, 17
"partner will change" attitude, 17
duality of the sexes, 191
"duty routine," 78
dynamic view of creation, 189

egocentrism
problems of, 21
ejaculation, 87
control of, 112
emotional conflict
with parents, 65
emotional preparation
woman's response to, 107
empathy
introspection of oneself, 54
escapist behavior, 46, 47
ethnocentrism
problem of, 50, 51

Fairchild, Roy W., 37
false principle of "right and wrong," 35
false sense of humor, 52
fear in communication, 59
female, purpose of, 190
finances
clarification of goals, 150
complicated by pregnancy, 151
conditioned feelings and attitudes, 148
controlling purse strings, 149
cooperative planning, 149
credit rating, 145, 146
credit related to employment, 146
credit costs, 146, 147
dealing with the unexpected, 152
dealing with variable costs, 152
double income, 151
facing up to bills, 144, 145
fixed costs, 150

focal point of tensions, 142, 143
honesty in financial dealings, 147
keeping in proper focus, 153
life style problems, 151
marital communication about, 147, 148
need for wise planning, 143
overextension of, 151
responsibility and debts, 144
review of spending plan, 149, 150
shopping for credit, 147
source of conflict, 144
uncertainty of tenure and seniority, 152
use of joint income, 149
use of spouse's skill, 148
variable costs, 150
wise use of savings and credit, 145
woman's contribution to, 149
five stages of marriage, 16, 17
flattery
as expression of love, 55
dishonesty in, 54, 55
forced change
consequences of, 13, 33
reasons for, 34
Freud, Sigmund, 108
frigidity
causes of, 102, 103

good communication, 39ff.
avoidance of, 43
examples of, 39ff.
honesty in everything, 42, 43
must be about everything, 43
restores
confidence, 42
trust, 41
understanding, 42
good fight
as constructive conflict, 47
characteristics of, 47, 48
need for, 45
good listening, 41
barriers to, 40, 41
guilt
attitude toward parents, 69
resolution of, 134

habitual patterns, 12
happily married men
characteristics of, 135, 136
happily married women
characteristics of, 135
happiness, 15
hostility
negative consequences, 47
hoax of extreme individualism, 204
humanity
and complementarity, 189, 190
mystery of, 191
humility in marriage, 37
hypocrisy in prayer, 36

improving communication, 50-60
where to start, 60
intelligent learning-listening, 41
intra-uterine device, 126, 127
"I was wrong—I am sorry," 23

Last Night of Don Juan, 204
life is dynamic, 15
listening
improvement of, 30, 31
problems of, 40ff.
love
basic routine for building, 26
Christian concept of, 16
"forgive and forget," 23
formula for building, 23
irresistible and unbreakable, 49
need for persistence, 22
need to express, 44
negative conditioning, 157
never fails, 22
no prerequisites, 22
problem of defining, 24
restoring reality, 23
toward parents, 69
love and sex
husband's role in, 103
love foreplay
importance of in marital sex, 111
love-making

perfection is achieved, 91
withholding love, 92

male, purpose of, 190
male as "sex fiend," 108
male-female sexual development, 100, 101
marital adjustment
game of "let's pretend," 47
"letdown" after marriage, 116
predetermined needs and expectations, 12
pressures, 11, 12
process involving time, 11
universal adaptations, 62
marital grievances
rank order of, 12, 13
marital sex
arousal of female, 84, 85
dealing with sex drive, 92, 93
love foreplay, 86
male as "sex fiend," 108
preparation for, 82
stimulation of clitoris, 86
timing and communication, 85
marital sexual communication, 104
marital success
perseverance necessary, 11
marriage
adjustment requirements, 63
attitude toward, 15
most important things going into it, 13, 62
mutual commitment, 11
significant attitudes, 11
viewed as process of becoming, 11
uniqueness of personalities, 61
mature love
couple creates, 21
search for definition, 16
maturity
accepting chronological age, 141
accepting inevitables, 141
adequate philosophy of life, 140
characteristics of, 140, 141
discernment of reality, 141
difference between child and adult, 30
economic reality, 143
independence and, 141
integration and, 140
not easily slighted, 141
objective toward self, 140
projection and, 134
respect for authority, 140, 141
suggestions accepted, 140
through communication with self, 28
meanings of sexual intercourse, 89ff.
menstruation, 95
modesty
affect on sex adjustment, 111
mutuality
beauty of, 23, 24
false sense of, 14
myths
automatic happiness in marriage, 15
"honeymoon idea," 17, 18
of compatibility, 13, 14
of males conquering women, 96
"silence is golden," 43
myth of motherhood, 63ff.
characteristics of "dear old mom," 63, 64
impact on marriage, 64ff.
mom and dad as humans, 64
myth surrounding marriage
"our marriage will be different," 12

nagging
as a habit pattern, 52
as immature behavior, 53, 54
barrier to communication, 52
definition, 53
forms of, 53
men as offenders, 53
negative conditioning of partner, 54
reasons for, 53
need for change
clinging to status, 74
fear of role change, 74

frankness, 73
habit of condemning people, 72
overly suspicious, 73, 74
perpetual worrier, 72
procrastination, 73
resenting evaluation, 71, 72
"running for shelter," 73
sarcastic digs, 72
underorganized, 71
need to build partner, 32
"no man is an island," 204

"one flesh," 78, 190, 191

perfect love story, 81ff.
permitting each other "to be," 139
personality faults and conflicts, 12ff.
personalization of relationships, 21
pill, 127, 128
"playboy philosophy," 80
destructive I-It relationship, 198
prayer in marriage
asking God to take over, 37
changes things, 35, 36
correct attitude toward, 36, 37
dictating to God, 37
humility in, 37
realism vs. unrealism, 37
understanding self in, 37
pre-ejaculation
how to deal with, 86
need for mutual understanding, 112
pregnancy
voluntary decision, 130
premarital sex
lessons from Scripture, 201, 202
psychological lessons, 202
sociological lessons, 202
traditional arguments, 187, 188
preparation for sexual intercourse
natural response, 111
patience required, 111
spontaneity, 111
pretending in communication, 42
problems
male attitude toward, 20
projection
as childish behavior, 134
examples of, 29, 30, 133, 134
immature response, 29
need to bring to conscious level, 30
psychological mechanism, 29
purpose of human existence, 203

quarreling, 43
attitudes toward, 45
constructive ways, 46
destructive ways, 46

real love
beginning of, 21
reason for marriage break-up, 49
resisting change, 71
resolving differences
deliberate act of will, 22
need for God's help, 22
respect for others, 138, 139
respect for parents, 68
responsible love, 188
responsibility
acceptance of, 133
failure to accept, 20, 21
retreatism, 19
"romantic myth," 12
rhythm method
cheating, 121
dealing with abstinence, 121, 122
factors causing irregular cycle, 121
fertility cycle, 120, 121
prerequisites for sexual fulfillment, 123
problems, 121, 122
reliability, 121
"self-sacrifice" and, 122
sex during the safe period, 123, 124
sexual frustrations of, 123
sexual needs and, 122
spontaneity and, 123

sarcasm
facing up to it, 52
false sense of humor, 52
how to detect, 52

satisfaction from minor virtues, 71
self-appraisal, 137, 138
self-love, importance of, 134
self-respect, 135
self-sacrifice
  confused with self-respect, 136, 137
  reality, 137
self-understanding
  developmental task, 70, 71
  questions to ask, 71
sensitivity to "the evil in others," 51
sex
  as end in itself, 80, 198
  as sacred marital duty, 78
  as sin, 77
  basic purpose of, 203
  Christian understanding of, 189, 190
  created in beauty, 109
  creation of persons, 190
  current misunderstanding, 77
  fear conditioning of, 95
  God's creation, 110
  God's plan for, 203
  humanization of, 189
  in behavioral terms, 80, 81
  involves total person, 80, 191
  "masculine right and feminine duty," 78
  mass media and, 79
  needs, 20
  no love-duty situation, 20
  no marriage without, 76
  "playboy philosophy" and, 80, 198
  pleasure-pain principle, 79
  problems of frustration of, 20
  reaction against tradition, 79
  "reward-punishment," 20
  right of "natural expression," 198
  romantic illusion, 79
  symbolic of commitment, 80
  "thou shalt not" approach, 92
  unrestricted, 79
  unwanted pregnancy and, 119, 120
sex education
  continuous process, 176
  facts and behavior, 182
  function of total personality, 181
  ignorance perpetuates mistakes, 178, 179
  importance of attitudes, 182
  involves God, 185
  limitations of "telling" process, 180
  love is basic, 174, 175
  love must be communicated in, 175
  myth and reality in, 178
  myth of "no sex education," 176
  need for parental confidence, 174
  negative learning, 177
  normal manner in, 184
  objectives in the home, 181
  parents' example in, 176, 177
  parents' experience and, 178
  parents' self-understanding, 178
  preventing trauma in, 183
  principles helpful to parents, 182ff.
  prudish modesty, 185
  simplicity in, 182, 183
  use of natural opportunities, 177
  weaknesses of, 179ff.
sex fulfillment for the female
  by-product of love, 101
sex outside of marriage
  biblical concepts, 189
  cheating of potential, 199
  denying wholeness to the other, 197, 198
  different from marital sex, 200
  does not meet needs, 200, 201
  experience not needed before marriage, 199
  freedom and self-fulfillment, 188
  frustrations and anxiety, 194, 195
  lacks continuity, 200
  leads to destructive concepts, 205
  loss of meaning, 196
  meaning and potential of, 194, 195
  no permanent relationship can be built, 200
  positive and negative contributions, 195
  questions to be asked, 187, 188
  response of many couples, 198, 199

sexual behavior not private, 204
solves no problems, 200
violation of dignity, 195
sexual adjustment
a continuing process, 76
bedroom as a place of love, 116, 117
expecting too much, or not enough, 76
female aggressiveness, 113
incomplete knowledge, 111
male's needs, 108, 109
menopause and, 115
merging of drives, 108
temptation to quit trying, 91
sexual decisions, 192-194
contraception and responsibility, 193, 194
demands, 193
environment as alibi, 193
self-control, 193
sexual deprivation
male feelings about, 107, 108
sexual development, 92ff.
sexual distortions, 77ff.
sexual frustration, 103, 104, 112
sexual fulfillment
during pregnancy, 114
during menopause, 115, 116
factors which limit, 114
levels of preparation, 107ff.
emotional, 107
physical, 107
spiritual, 107
no short cuts to, 199, 200
pre-menstrual tensions, 115
sexual intercourse
anxiety about virility, 99
brings profound change, 197
dignity of in marriage, 109
effect of alcohol, 109, 110
emotional preparation for, 82
hedonistic illusion, 198
importance of initial relationship, 91
involves the total being, 197
male awareness in, 83, 84
motions of, 87
myth of deep penetration, 98, 99
need for experimentation, 100
need for privacy, 116
no "sin" in the bedroom, 116, 117
"not what you do, what you are," 87
physical cleanliness, 116
physical preparation for, 82
position of, 87
process of, 83, 84
spiritual act, 109
symbolic of commitment, 196
taboos and inhibitions, 111
techniques, 85
"to know," 192, 197
unique knowledge about another, 196, 197
sexual learning
assumption of virginity, 97
attitudes toward menstruation, 95
attitudes toward pregnancy, 94, 95
bad information, 98
conditioned-in fears, 97
"I-It" relationship, 96
"I know everything" myth, 96, 97
masculine myth, 95, 96
myths from marriage manuals, 99, 100
parents' attitudes, 93
"wifely duty," 94
sexual mutuality, 117
sexual responsibility, 193
sexual signals, 82
sexual stimulation
sensitive female areas, 110
sexual "triggers"
clitoris, 86
penis, 83
sexual union
most vital of all communication, 192
not an isolated act, 192
total involvement of personality, 192
SIECUS study guide, 181

simultaneous climax, 84
idealized, 107
sources of sexual facts, 174
special sexual tensions, 114, 115
Steinmetz, Urban G., 121
stereotyped female sexual role, 113
"strong silent type," 57, 58
successful marriage
need to build your partner, 32
no magic formulas, 16
permitting our partner "to be," 32

tensions
destroy communication, 18
early in marriage, 18
Terman, L. M., 12, 135
"time of awakening"
beginning of mature love, 21
concentration on happiness of the other, 22
concern for remodeling abandoned, 22
deliberate act of will, 21, 22
marriage as real, 21
making it work, 21
taking a look at oneself, 21
"time of disillusion"
communication deteriorates, 18
doubts, 18
feelings of not being loved, 18, 19
rigidity and inflexibility, 18
seeing marriage as "it really is," 18
tensions, 18
"time of love"
acceptance of person, 22
beautiful phase, 22
communications restored, 23
"I was wrong-I am sorry," 23
no prerequisites, 22
partner loved as "he is," 23
sex more meaningful, 23, 24
"time of misery"
absence of hope, 19
communication absent, 19
divorce, 19
no real attempts to move back, 20, 21
sex is dead, 20
sex as "reward-punishment," 19, 20
solving one's own problems, 20
togetherness, false sense of, 14
total climax of love, 106ff.
Christian perspective, 107
trust in marriage, 139

unhappily married men
characteristics of, 136
unhappily married women
characteristics of, 135
Upper Peninsula Family Enrichment Bureau, 121

"wifely duty," 94
woman's love needs, 102
woman's needs, 108